Stranger at the Pentagon

by
Frank E. Stranges, Ph.D.

(Fourth Revised Edition)

COPYRIGHT © 1991 Dr. Frank E. Stranges
All Rights Reserved
1st Printing 1967
2nd Printing 1967
3rd Printing 1972 (Third Revised Edition)
4th Printing 1991 (Special Fourth Revised Edition)
Published by: **INNER LIGHT PUBLICATIONS**
P.O. Box 753
New Brunswick, N.J. 08903
ISBN—0-938-294-66-0

STRANGER AT THE PENTAGON

Dr. Frank E. Stranges

FRANK E. STRANGES, PH.D.

> Wisdom is the principle thing
> therefore get Wisdom.
> And with all thy getting...
> Get understanding.
> Proverbs 4:7

STRANGER AT THE PENTAGON

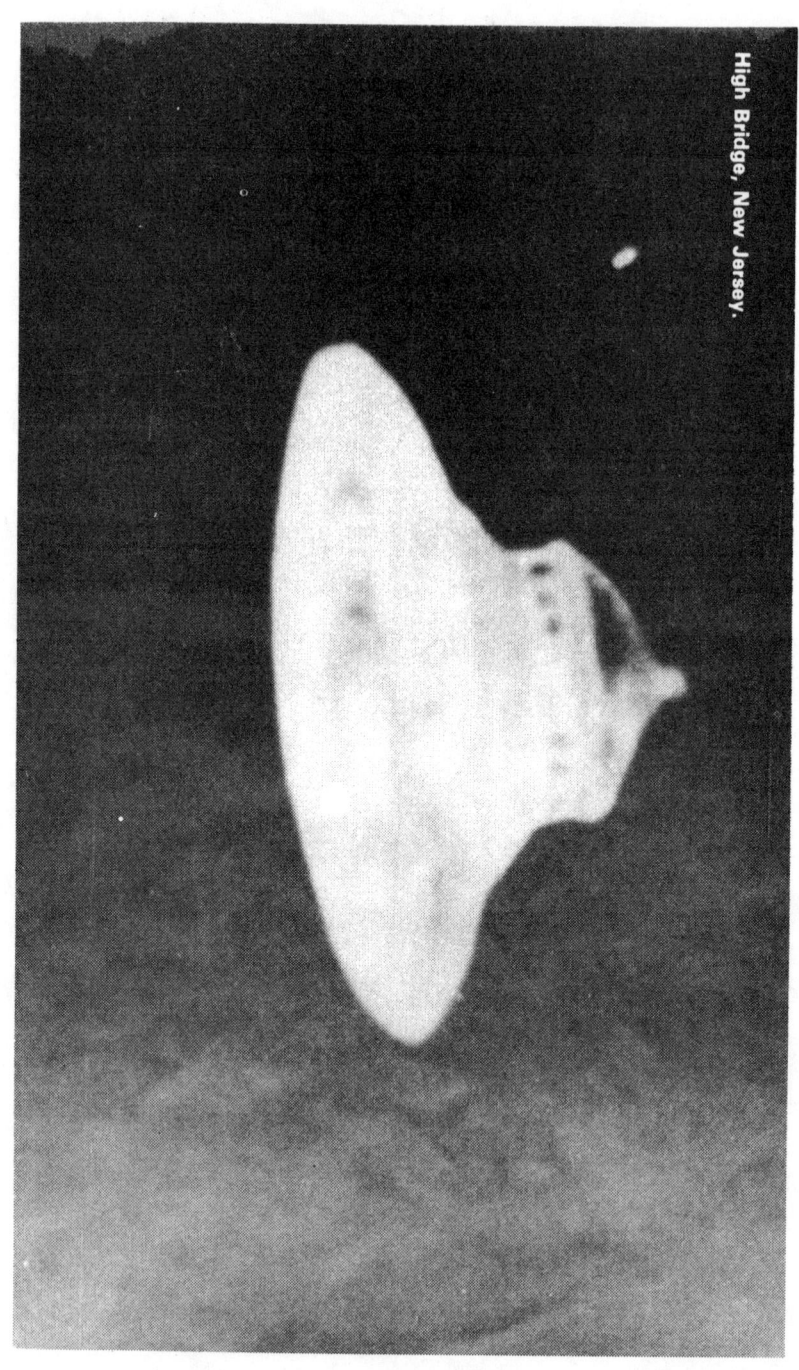

High Bridge, New Jersey.

Frank E. Stranges, Ph.D.

Table of Contents

ONE
THE LANDING .... Page 23

TWO
THE MEETINGS BEGIN .... Page 49

THREE
A LIFE SPARED .... Page 55

FOUR
WELCOME ABOARD .... Page 65

FIVE
VAL'S APPOINTMENT TO COMMANDER .... Page 79

SIX
THE AIRPORT ATTACK .... Page 85

SEVEN
THE RING OF FIRE .... Page 93

EIGHT
SPACECRAFT OVER EARTH .... Page 103

EPILOGUE .... Page 117

A FINAL WORD FROM VAL THOR .... Page 121

SIGNS AND WONDERS .... Page 125

UFOs are frequently seen
over Pyramids of Egypt.

About the Author

DR. FRANK E. STRANGES is Founder/President of the NATIONAL INVESTIGATIONS COMMITTEE ON UFOs. In addition, he is President of International Evangelism Crusades (a world-wide Christian Denomination) and International Theological Seminary of California. He was born in New York and educated in Brooklyn, Pennsylvania, Minnesota and California. He holds degrees in Theology, Psychology and Criminology.

During the past forty-four years, he has investigated various facets of the UFO phenomena and has authored many books on the subject. His interest began while he was attending Bible College after hearing his roommate tell of an experience during the War. He was told that the squadron in which his roommate was flying was buzzed by several UFOs and during the "debriefing", the pilots were told they had seen nothing unusual. After confirming the story personal with the other members of the flight team, Dr. Stranges began serious inquiry into the fascinating subject of UFOs.

Dr. Stranges is an Assistant Deputy Director of the California State Marshal's Association and a Chaplain of the American Federation of Police. Numerous affiliations with law enforcement, scientific, religious and public service organizations attest to his dedication to Community Service. His University and College presentations are recognized as an important contribution to the understanding of the truth about the UFO phenomena today.

Acknowledgments

The author wishes to express his sincere thanks to Mr. August C. Roberts, one of the foremost photographers in the U.F.O. field, whose photographs appear in this and prior editions.

ALSO

My deepest thanks to Robert Hover, Editor-Publisher-Author, for his keen insight revealed in his contribution to this volume. Mr. Hover is indeed one of the few men in this generation who sustain the ability to receive truth and light as few men do today. When one reads his contribution, one knows beyond question that his information has not originated from an Earthly source.

This book is dedicated to Julie A. Corcoran, whose unselfish efforts helped greatly in the separation of fact from fiction and who spent many, many hours "perfecting the vehicle" before it has been placed in your hands.

My one true love, this is for you.

Dr. Harley Byrd

Forward

By Harley Andrew Byrd

Frank E. Stranges, Ph.D.

The Val Thor Landing
002741-57 Room 4D-717
Project Blue Book

During the winter of 1956-57, the Washington, D.C. area was extremely cold, but it was a good feeling to be working in a high security position in the Pentagon. I lived only a short distance away in Georgetown, the old section of the Nation's Capitol. Senator J.F. Kennedy lived on "O" Street just a block away from our house on Prospect. During a successful tour with the U.S. Naval Ceremonial Honor Guard, we had met with astronauts Glenn, Cooper, Wally Sherrar, who were the first wave of successful space travelers. Also we had visited the Tomb of the Unknown Soldier numerous times. It seemed like every time a visiting dignitary came to Washington, they lay a wreath at the tomb. We had met the Queen of England several times at the airport, as these were some of the duties I performed as a young officer in the Navy. After carrying the 2-Star flag at the funeral of my late uncle, Rear Admiral Richard E. Byrd, I was recommended for a security clearance and was granted a Top Secret Clearance after a lengthy six-month background study (B1 complete 1957). After being transferred to the Chief of Naval Information (CHINFO), I worked in the Security Clearance section before being indoctrinated into the branch office of the Air Force called PROJECT BLUE BOOK. It was a joint service office; that is, two Marines, two Army, two Navy and three Air Force officers.

The work was routine, opening incoming mail, sorting

out what was called actual sightings as opposed to many fake UFO photos. We also acted as a Public Information Office (PIO), much like a public relations office. Every publisher's dream was to get the real low down on the UFO situation, which was suppressed by the group that dictated national policy on the UFO matter.

In mid March, 1957, we received an urgent message from the Alexandria Police Department. The message indicated that two of their on-duty police officers had picked up an alien who had landed some 14 miles south of Pentagon Boulevard, and the occupant was transported to the Pentagon to meet with the Under Secretary of Defense and then shuttled underground to meet with President Eisenhower and Vice President Richard Nixon. The meeting lasted for nearly an hour and then, the alien visitor was put on VIP status and was shuttled back to the Pentagon where he spent the night in the Army reception office on the first floor near the concourse. This alien's name was Valiant Thor.

Commander James was on duty at the Security Clearance and Review for the branch officer of the Project Blue Book. He oversaw the meeting through official channels and reported the landing and meeting of the "space emissary", as he was labeled by the Department of Defense, to a governing group of high military officials including Secretary of Defense D.F. Forestall and other scientific men of which there were twelve. They in turn made recommendations to the President and Cabinet members, the CIA, FBI, NSA and so on. The landing of Valiant Thor was perhaps the first documented landing of a human-type alien by military officials. He contacted an individual in the Pentagon who was an advocate of the UFO alien situation. "Nancy Warren" in turn contacted a minister, who was also a private investigator and theologian, a Dr. Frank E. Stranges, who then met with this individual. Dr. Stranges had been a guest speaker at the National Evangelistic Center for two weeks.

Val Thor landed in Alexandria and met with the President to discuss the world's problems and offer advice and counsel on how to deal with and eliminate them. He indicated to Mr. Eisenhower that the world was in a precarious situation and that if the world continued to proceed on a war footing—which Val Thor felt would be a self-destruct mode—it would cause an economic imbalance throughout the world. Val Thor stayed on Earth until March 16, 1960, and then disembarked to his home planet Venus. He indicated that his race of people lived and dwelled underground and that many of the planets throughout the universe sustain life in this same manner. He also mentioned the waves of aliens who would land around the world to help with the Earth's seemingly unsurmountable problems. He stated that a group from a distant planetary system would be coming to give aid and data to help the Earth's progress. Val Thor spoke of Christ's presence in the universe and that it was heartwarming to see Christ's advanced teaching continuing. This visitation at the Pentagon marks perhaps a new era in knowledge, wisdom and understanding on our planet.

> Harley Andrew Byrd
> Nephew to the late
> Rear Admiral Richard R.E. Byrd,
> United States Navy

Introduction

It was while I was attending Seminary School that I first heard about what were then being called "Flying Saucers," and while others around me might have laughed, I felt I had an open mind and sincerely wanted to learn the truth.

What I found was that astute men of authority had gone on record as being among those in the world that have admitted the presence and reality of the unidentified flying objects.

Men such as Captain Eddie Rickenbacker, who said "Flying saucers are real...too many good men have seen them, men that do not have hallucinations."

Henry J. Taylor asserts that during his research to determine whether "Flying Saucers" actually do exist, and if so, where they have come from, "I was actually stumped by the conflicting reports of eyewitnesses, until I found there are two mysteries in our skies instead of one." One mystery involves our development of secret weapons: but the other is not revealed by an "earthly interpretation."

Air Chief Marshall Lord Dowding, command in chief of the Royal Air Force, stated, "I am convinced that these objects do exist. They are not manufactured by any nation of this earth."

The United States Air Force to this date has denied the very existence of flying saucers. Therefore, the term unidentified flying objects has been introduced and carried through. They evidently are not too certain as to the whys and wherefores...or do they???

The late Major Donald Keyhoe, the renowned director of the National Investigations Committee on Aerial Phenomena, made a thorough investigation of this subject. Major Keyhoe, as a result of his investigation, offered much information. He stated that flying discs actually change colors in the sky, and it has been proven. To affirm this he states, "During daytime periods, scores of metallic-looking discs, have been seen to change color during maneuvers. One typical report, in 1950, described an encounter near Lewisburg, West Virginia. Two round, silvery discs, had approached the city, then swung into a tight, fast circle. As the maneuvers began, both turned orange-red. When they straightened, reducing speed, the orange quickly faded and the discs resumed their normal silvery color.

Also, be informed of the following event involving Captain Robert Adickes, a stocky ex-Navy pilot with ten years service with the TWA. I refer to the dramatic incident near South Bend, Indiana. On the night of April 27, 1950 at 8:25 P.M., with Captain Adickes in the left hand seat of a TWA DC-3, over on the right, sat Robert F. Manning, also a four-stripe Captain, who was acting as first officer on this flight to Chicago. The DC-3, Flight 117, was cruising at 20,000 feet when a strange, red light below and behind the airliner suddenly caught Mannings eye. Puzzled, Manning, watched it close in...the light steadily growing in size. It was now an orange-red color, like a blob of hot metal sweeping through the night sky. Craning his neck, Manning looked down on a spherical shape which glowed brightly on top, its lower half in shadow...To Adickes it looked like a huge red wheel rolling down a road. He banked toward it, but the discs instantly slid away, keeping the same distance. Again he tried, with the same results. Calling the hostess, Gloria Hinshaw, Adickes told her to alert the passengers, to make sure he had plenty of witnesses."

A report on the type of men the pilots were from the TWA offices, described them both as "Quiet...conservative...serious... careful." Nobody in TWA questioned that Adickes and Manning had seen exactly what they had said. Gloria Hinshaw had seen the disc from the cabin, and the pilot's cockpit. She told Major Keyhoe, "It looked like a big red wheel rolling along"; she also made the statement that "on top it looked like it was on fire." Major Keyhoe interviewed all 11 passengers by long distance calls. The first one being S.N. Miller, manager of a jewelry company in St. Paul. He had watched the saucer for several minutes. He accounted for it, saying, "The thing was the color of a neon sign —not just a big red disc. I used to laugh at saucer stories, but not any more."

Major Keyhoe said that "among other passengers who confirmed the sighting, were C.H. Jenkins, and D.c. Bourland, engineers with the Boeing Aircraft Co., and E.J. Fitzgerald, V.P. of a metal equipment corporation in Chicago. Later several officials of the International Harvester Company also admitted they had seen the glowing disc as it paced the plane."

More reports of their fiery red appearance come from Greenville, S.C., where on the night of May 13, 1952, astronomers had seen four saucers flying...glowing a reddish yellow (amber). On June 19, 1952, intelligence reports came from Goose Bay Air Force Base that "a glowing red disc approached the field at night."

There is absolutely no question whatever concerning the actual existence of these flying objects. There is certainly something...in the skies above us and someone...is responsible for them being there. It has been stated time and again that these objects "must" be under intelligent control.

One of the greatest "thorns in the flesh" to many Bible scholars, ministers, etc., is the statement of "Life on other Planets." It seems very strange that we who are "Finite Beings" continually attempt to force God into the test tube of our two by four human understanding and reasoning. We must never lose sight of the one prime fact that "God is the Creator" while we are His creation.

During the past few years, I have met men and women from all walks of life. Many of these people are continually looking for truth. Seeking for the very truths that will cause a better way of life to come up over the far horizon. Nevertheless, if we can but place our trust in God, and lay hold on the blessings and provisions that are made for us through the Lord Jesus Christ, we might make the discovery that these great "revelations" are with the grasp of every honest believer.

In the following pages, as you carefully study the questions and answers supplied me by this friend from outer space, you will find that...unlike many other "contact stories," Val does not minimize the fact that Jesus Christ is the first and the last, the alpha and the omega, and the beginning and the end.

That is one great reason why I believe that Val has spoken the truth and nothing but the truth concerning his mission to this wayward planet.

• • •

Often, events transpire that cause one to wonder if these

certain events really happened or are figments of the imagination. Then, one begins to ponder the facts that have caused an experience to really "live".

Writing this book has presented quite a challenge. The following is an account as told to me and which involved the Earth visits of one, Valiant Thor, from another planet. The story itself is quite unique. Many have read of this unusual visit at the Pentagon and have likewise claimed to have first-hand information that this event did in fact take place. At the same time, there are those who choose to accept this account as something that could not possibly have taken place because of the intense security at the Pentagon. Then again, there are those who would retort that the Pentagon is the ONLY PLACE this could have happened.

It will be most interesting to continue watching this account develop over the coming years. Although these incidents took place beginning in 1957, they have reportedly been witnessed by many others in many parts of the world. Some of these witnesses have related the incidents while others have chosen to remain silent because of the fear of ridicule. They would never think of openly repeating their own experiences with one claiming to be from another world.

Valiant addressed a special group of representatives at the United Nations in a closed session. The ramifications of such a gathering forced the exclusion of the media from this meeting. He appeared of his own free will. The delegates were stunned, some to the point of anger, some to the point of fear.

He is on a special mission to this third planet from the

Sun and is presently working with many hundreds of his "crew" in conjunction with many on this planet.

The following pages will reveal much...at least to those who are capable of discerning knowledge, wisdom and above all, understanding. As you read through the pages, you will find yourself caught up in the story itself. Some of you will read with great delight and desire. Others will read with an eye to ridicule. However, as you read, you must certainly agree that during the past sixty years, we have come a very long way in the related fields of science and technology. As you continue to read, please remember that any decision you choose is entirely up to you. Strive to maintain an open mind. The things that we think we know, we do not know at all...while the things we do not know are oftimes revealed to us surrounded by pure golden light...thus enlarging our capability to believe.

This might well be the year that UFOs will prove once and for all that we are not alone in this expanding universe and that we, members of the human family, might conceivably learn that our family ties are not restricted to this planet Earth. Remember, you are never alone.

To those who have the eyes to see and the ears to hear, I say God bless you...to all others, God help you.

DR. FRANK E. STRANGES
1991

Chapter One
The Landing

"Hello, Frank, how are you?" That greeting will forever be etched in my memory. It always brings me back to that cold day in December, 1959, a day which changed my life forever and one which I will recall as if it were yesterday for the rest of my life. That day began a journey which continues and one which endures even to this writing.

The story began centuries ago with the first reconnaissance exploration voyage which confirmed that there indeed was life on this third planet from the Sun...

There had been occasions which presented a dilemma to both the "observed" as well as the "observer". These included several pilots being "beamed" into the ship in order to save their lives. This was a far cry from the first incidents of men throwing rocks in an attempt to repel the ship. It was during 1945 that the Earth was surrounded by 100 ships in order to protect the fragile atmosphere which surrounds it. A chain atomic reaction could easily have resulted because of the separation of the elements of the air. Earth could have been destroyed thus creating many problems, a ripple effect so to speak, throughout the universe.

After reporting the observations of various voyages, several recommendations were made. The first was that an aerial display be performed in order to provide evidence of the physical existence of life, as it is known here, on other planets in the solar system.

This was accomplished during the Truman Administration over the Capitol Building in Washington, D.C.

Newspapers reported the occurrence complete with details of "the chase". What they didn't report was that the

UFOs were not visible below the planes which had been sent up...they were only visible to those on the ground.

The second recommendation was for physical contact with world leaders, beginning with the United States.

The First Meeting

March 16, 1957, in Alexandria, Virginia, one of the finest leaders of the planet Venus, operating under the direction of the Central Control and who had been chosen to make the contact as well as direct the project, landed his craft and was met by two police officers, weapons drawn. A thought transference quickly convinced them that he meant no harm and he was ushered into the back seat of their patrol car. After crossing over into Washington, D.C., they were met by the Secretary of Defense along with six of his staff members. Soon police from every conceivable district and agency had joined in, all trying to claim their right to escort him to President Dwight D. Eisenhower. Through his own version of the power of positive thinking, he was able to dismiss them all and soon passed through the security posts followed by an Air Force Captain.

Meanwhile, his presence in the area had thrown everyone into a dilemma. The introduction he held from the High Council worried them because, though not written in any Earthly language, their minds were given power to properly translate the inscribed message. Captain Gould (not his real name) asked him to remain and after downing two plain bourbons muttered...

"My god, why couldn't this have happened on my day off?"

Valiant Thor

Val with writing tablet.

Suddenly the door opened and six armed guards led Val to what appeared to be an elevator. It went rapidly to the bottom-most level. Maximum security was in place. After transferring to an underground train, they sped toward the White House. Six officials, six armed guards and three secret service men escorted him into the office of President Eisenhower.

From behind the desk the President rose while the secret service men remained nervous and uneasy. As he extended his hand to shake that of the President, the secret service men drew their revolvers and pointed them at Val. Following the nod of the President, they reluctantly lowered their guns.

Standing in front of his desk, the President said, "Of course, you know we have suspended all rules of protocol. I have a good feeling toward you. Please, sir, what is your name?"

He replied, "Valiant."

"And where do you come from?"

"I come from the planet your Bible calls the morning and the evening star."

"Venus?"

"Yes, sir."

"Can you prove this," he asked.

"What do you constitute as proof?"

He quickly retorted, "I don't know."

"Will you come with me to my ship?"

He answered with a quizzical look and said, "My friend, I cannot come and go as I please. There are others to be considered. There are committees to be consulted and security measures to be adhered to. Please spend some time with us here...Let's get better acquainted...learn more about one

Val and friends at backyard meeting in High Bridge, New Jersey.

Val, Donn, Jill, Tanyia.

Frank E. Stranges, Ph.D.

Val, Jill, Donn.

another...and perhaps soon, real soon, well...we shall see."

Richard Nixon

At that moment, another gentleman rushed into the room. It turned out to be Vice President Richard Nixon. He appeared to Val to be very sharp, quick-witted, with fixed eyes and an amazing aptitude toward speed and proficiency.

"My name is Valiant," he said as the Vice President thrust his hand without hesitation.

"You have certainly caused a stir...for an out of towner." The Vice President smiled as he continued, "Of course, we are not totally convinced of anything just yet. But suffice it to say we are checking and double checking everything you say and do. When Sergeant Young from Alexandria radioed in and stated that you had just landed in a flying saucer, we thought," he continued, "Sergeant Young had flipped. Say, were you in on that UFO flap over Washington? You certainly had us all in a dither, if you were."

After assuring them that this planet had been under close scrutiny for hundreds of years before the 1945 bomb blast and with his special letter still in the slightly quivering hand of the President, he was requested to follow the Secret Service back the way they had come...to the Pentagon and into a beautifully furnished apartment where he would spend the next three years. Fortunately, he was prepared for such a lengthy visit and kept in constant communication with the Starship. There were many occasions during which he teleported himself in and out of those quarters often exercising "trans-imagery" to cause the security guards to visualize his face on a nonexistent I.D. badge.

Photos Taken

Soon after his arrival, together with three members of his crew, he joined a "convention" in the back yard of the home of Mr. Howard Menger in High Bridge, New Jersey. The month was April, 1957. A certain group of individuals who were interested in UFOs were meeting that day. Val and his crew members, Donn, Jill and Tanyia, had changed into the same type of clothing worn by their Earth friends. The meeting was very interesting and these people were on the right track. He was dismayed to learn the undignified manner in which these people were treated by the press. Nevertheless, these people were pursuing their beliefs and this was good. A curious young photographer, August C. Roberts, snapped several pictures, thinking he was doing so without Val's knowledge. The photographer seemed to be greatly troubled when he attempted to talk to him. Yet, it was those very photographs which were to bring me together with this unusual man on that cold December day.

Holding the message from the High Council in his hand, the President stated that Val's offer to help the human family would upset the economy of the United States and could plunge her into the abyss of chaos. In brief, he politely told Val that the people of this planet were not ready to cope with such conditions as would come into existence if the recommendations of this unearthly visitor were put into action. Nevertheless, he was invited to assist a number of scientists who were out working on medical projects directly associated with the space sciences. His allotted time to acquaint the leaders of the United States with his suggestions was limited to three years. During this time, he refused to advise them regarding a certain "bomb in the sky" which we now know as the Star Wars system.

"Miracle" Garment

In his apartment, he was able to maintain communications with his ship and was kept informed of the growing world tensions. His uniform underwent rigid tests at that time. By today's standards, they would now be obsolete. They attempted to penetrate the material with a diamond drill bit, but it snapped under pressure. Acid rolled off the uniform and burned a hole in the floor. They fired a high-velocity rifle at the uniform but it failed to pierce it. The report to the President read:

Physical appearance—Soft silver and gold lustrous

Fabric—Unknown

Weight—Six ounces, total, including boots

Cut—Close fitting like a tunic; no cuffs, pockets, buttons, zippers, clips or hooks

RXT-2 Tests—Indestructible

Finally, a bright-eyed Colonel escorted him to a place where the final test would be performed. Val looked at the laser instrument amusingly. Upon command, the laser aimed a fine line of intense light amplification by stimulated emission of radiation. The Colonel began his discourse that this device contained a crystal-synthetic ruby in which atoms, when stimulated by focused light waves, amplify and concentrate these waves, then emit the beam. As the Colonel continued to speak, his smile gave way to utter dismay... the ray being totally ineffective against the garment. He babbled on

Valiant Thor holding papers.

long after the laser has been turned off. He reiterated how powerful the U.S. had become since the splitting of the atom. He gave Val a lesson in atomic fusion. He went on to state that when a chain reaction of nuclear fission is set off by a neutron bombardment in the atoms or a charge of plutonium or uranium isotope with an atomic weight of 235 (U-235), an immense quantity of energy is suddenly released. The good Colonel finally talked himself out and Val was conducted back to his quarters...along with his uniform.

1959 was fast drawing to a close. Chiefs of State were in a constant turmoil and confusion was the rule of the day. Indecision caused delay after delay. Economists and industrial giants conferred with politicians and military heads daily. The Government leaders could not reconcile Val's being in a position to force their hand if he so desired. Several scientists attempted to learn the secrets of interstellar travel...without success.

Christmas week was now upon us. I had been busily presenting a series of scientific lectures and speaking at a number of Churches in Washington, D.C. Earlier that month, I had returned from Cuba where I met personally with Fidel Castro.

Unbeknownst to me, Val, working with "Nancy Warren" (she was one of only a few since his arrival at the Pentagon in whom he was able to discern an honest and open heart and who loved Almighty God, her country and her fellow man), formulated a plan whereby I would be contacted.

Inside the Pentagon

Many Earth people live one life openly while in their

hearts and minds, they live quite another. Doublemindedness seemed to be a way of life in the Pentagon building that served as the busy nerve center of our nation. Val once remarked to me that he had never witnessed in one central location such concentrated confusion.

"Nancy" attended the lecture/service which I conducted at the National Evangelistic Center, pastored by Dr. John Mears, in Washington, D.C. Following the conclusion of my talk, she approached the platform and asked to speak to me. Strangely enough, the photographer in New Jersey had given Val's photographs to me and I had been displaying them at my lectures ever since. I had no personal knowledge of them, other than what I had been told by the photographer. When she was unable to "grab" my attention while I was signing copies of my book SAUCERAMA, she showed her Pentagon ID and that got my attention quickly to say the least.

We borrowed the Pastor's study and she asked me if I would like to meet the man in the photographs personally. Of course, I answered her with a resounding yes. She then asked if I could follow instructions to the letter, to which I replied that I could, and she told me to meet her at the curb in front of my hotel at 8:00 A.M. the next morning.

"Nancy" arrived precisely on time and thus began the journey which at times would seen unreal, but which later would prove beyond doubt that there is truly life in God's Universe.

Those of you familiar with the Pentagon know that the normal traffic flow approaching it is to the right. We drove to the left. I knew then that something strange was going on.

We had to stand in line to pass by a security guard. First one, then the second, "VISUALIZED" an identification badge on my lapel. This utterly amazed me and I felt that at any minute, I would be picked up, handcuffed and thrown into some jail somewhere. This of course was only my imagination and anticipation of what was about to take place. "Nancy" left me standing in front of a door which contained no markings.

As the door opened, I walked in and stood on the threshold. My stocky form shifted from one foot to the other as I cleared my throat. The three men in the room were completely unaware of my presence and ignored me. I was puzzled to say the least. Later, I would find out that Val had clouded their minds and rendered them oblivious to the entire session. They continued with their work.

The Stranger Appears

Being a minister of the Gospel of Jesus Christ, as well as a student of the Bible for many years, coupled with my experience as an special investigator, I felt as though my senses were functioning properly and that I knew exactly what I was about to do. I was on my guard for fakes and frauds. In walked a man, about six feet tall, perhaps 185 pounds, brown wavy hair, brown eyes. His complexion appeared normal and slightly tanned. As I approached him and he looked at me IT WAS AS THOUGH HE LOOKED STRAIGHT THROUGH ME. With a warm smile and extending his hand, he greeted me by name.

"Hello, Frank. How are you?"

His genuineness astonished me, but quickly I understood.

As I gripped his hand, I was somewhat surprised to feel the soft texture of his skin...like that of a baby but with the strength of a man that silently testified to his power and intensity.

His voice was very strong and mellow. It was filled with purpose and character. I again looked around the room to see whether the other men would say or do anything. They were still working as if I weren't there.

I noticed that he was wearing the same type of clothing as I. When I asked if he possessed any other clothing, he said that he had given several officials a garment so that they could run tests on it. He then proceeded to a closet and produced a one-piece "suit" that glittered as the sun which streamed in through the window hit the fabric. I thought that it looked like liquid sunshine. I asked him about the material from which it was made.

He answered, "It is made of a material not of this Earth."

The general appearance of the suit was all one piece...even down to the boots. It contained no buttons, zippers or snaps. I asked him how it held together. He demonstrated by holding the front together and passing his hand over it as if to smooth it out. I could not even locate the opening. It was held together by an invisible force.

To Help Mankind

He told me that his purpose in coming was to help mankind return to the Lord. He spoke in positive terms...always with a smile on his face. He said that man was further away from God than ever before, but there was still a good chance if man looks in the right place. He told me he had been here nearly three years and would depart in just a few months. Claiming that he would not use force to speak with men in authority in America, he was happy to consult with them at their invitation. He further stated that thus far only a few men in Washington knew of his existence in the Pentagon. And few leaders had availed themselves of his advice during these past three years. He felt there was still so much to do and yet his time of departure was getting near. He told me that Jesus Christ would not force men to be saved from their mistakes, even though He had already made a way for mankind to be redeemed through His shed blood.

When I asked him where he was from, he replied, "I am from the Planet that is called Venus."

I asked him how many visitors from Venus were presently on Earth and he said, "There are presently seventy-seven of us walking among you in the United States. We are constantly coming and going."

During the next thirty minutes, he told me things about myself that even I did not know. Later, I was able to verify them with my parents and grandparents. He gave me information regarding the gravitational pull of Venus in comparison to Earth. I was informed that the abdominal muscles hold flesh firm against the mild gravitational pull, which is three-twentieths less than that of Earth. He gave me information which would be revealed to others over a period of years.

No Fingerprints

The only thing he said that troubled me was his use of the expression "when the time is right" in response to my question as to whether or not I would see him again. His lack of fingerprints intrigued me as I had been involved as a private investigator for quite some time, even working at times on loan to some of the Government agencies. I had learned the science of fingerprints...with the impression of the lines and whorls on the inner surface of the last joint of each finger on the human hand. He told me that all Earth people were thusly marked since the fall of Adam in the Garden of Eden, during the very dawn of civilization as we know it today.

He began to prepare me for the road which lie ahead. It would not be an easy one..There would be adversities, organized attempts to both discourage and discredit me, but the rewards have proved to outweigh these trials which continue even to this day.

We discussed the merits of Jesus Christ...how He gave His Life freely...so that men could enjoy the benefits of eternal life. I questioned him about a Bible on Venus and he assured me that a personal unbroken fellowship with the "Author" did not necessitate the printing of a "book". He found it amusing that many theologians attempt to discredit both Jesus Christ and The Bible. The very God many have said is "dead" continues to lavish them with all good things. Perhaps they will, in time, permit the spark of Divine Light to again illuminate their troubled hearts.

In answer to my question of what he thought of Jesus Christ, he said, "I know that Jesus is the Alpha and Omega of yours and everyone else's faith. He today has assumed His rightful position as the ruler of the universe and is preparing a place and a time for all who are called by His Name to ascend far above the clouds to where His Power and Authority shall never again be disputed.

"I believe that Jesus Christ is the wonder of wonders and changes not. No, not forever and forever."

As he spoke these words, my own heart burned within me and tears filled my eyes.

He turned to the window and said, "Frank, it will not be long. Contend for the faith, and you will never miss the mark.

I asked him if there is life on other planets.

Life on Other Planets

His reply was, "There is life on many other planets of which people on Earth know nothing. There are more solar systems for which man has not even given God credit. There are many beings that have never transgressed the perfect laws of God. Man does not possess the right to condemn the whole of God's creation because he himself has broken the perfect laws of God through disobedience."

I asked him what he would do if the military prevented him from leaving on the appointed day.

He simply stated, "Frank, do you remember one day after Jesus arose from the dead, He had gone in search of several of His followers? They closed themselves in a locked room and suddenly they saw Jesus standing in the very midst of them?"

He then smiled and looked at me as if to imply, "Need I say more?"

As I turned to leave the room, he said simply, "Please keep your faith and leave the same way that you came in. Continue to seek first the Kingdom of God and His Righteousness and all other things will, in time, be added to you and yours. Goodbye for now and God bless you and keep you always."

I left that meeting astounded, greatly encouraged, and yet with a heavy heart, not knowing what the future would hold. I began to wonder who would believe me if I ever told of this strange encounter with a man from another planet. I first considered not repeating this extraordinary story, but the more I thought about it, the more I prayed about it, the more I felt that it would bring a great blessing to those who would hear and read it.

This interplanetary traveler possessed a wealth of knowledge, not only about science and God, but also about me. He stated that my book SAUCERAMA could not have been written without Heavenly guidance.

Val's instructions were to leave Washington, D.C., no later than March 16, 1960. That meant that there were less than three months during which he could confer with scientists, politicians, military men and the like. All missed his point entirely. They were all filled with self-ambition and cared little for the pressing needs of mankind. His efforts to bring about an end to the sickness and disease that plague this planet were met with pathetic refusal. He was told over and over that his presence and his ideas were a threat to the political and economic structure. Certain religious leaders were also fearful of losing a grip on the people in the event that his presence was admitted on an official level. It was very disheartening that the administration failed to lay hold of such information that would change the course of human activities for the good...because of economic reasons.

Security regulations were very tight, but despite the fact

that they knew he would come and go as he pleased, they delighted in playing their game. Val had vowed not to use force and so another course of action would be necessary if the information which he had to relate were to be disseminated. This is the reason why he contacted men of Godly character and strength around the world. Many are presently working in close contact with Val and other members of his crew.

Meeting with President

His last meeting with the President did not reap any lasting results. He wanted to let the world know of Val's proposed plan, but the Secretary of Defense, the head of the Central Intelligence Agency and the Military Chiefs of Staff were opposed to his suggestion. The President attempted to effect a joint meeting before the General Assembly of the United Nations. But this plan too was rejected. He was informed that the U.N. would receive a special "press release" in the form of a memorandum to the Secretary General no later than February 7, 1966. These leaders of the U.S. Government argued long into the night, fearing that if the people of this nation learned of the plan Val was offering, they might choose to follow him instead of them. When a man feels that his personal peace and tranquility may be threatened, the human reaction is always that of swift self-preservation. At one point, the Vice President insisted that the "pressure boys" allow the President to make the choice. He was vetoed without even a chance to complete his statements.

CIA Secret Files

Frank E. Stranges, Ph.D.

World conditions were not growing any better. Much international pressure was being brought to bear upon the administration. They fought diligently and enforced rigid regulations with stiff penalties for revealing Val's presence. Even a major newscaster who inadvertently learned of his visit through one of his paid informants was silenced by none other than the Central Intelligence Agency, which has consistently disclaimed all knowledge concerning UFOs. Meanwhile, they maintain secret files that could actually prove the existence of intelligent life in the universe beyond all doubt.

The morning of March 15, 1960 saw Val meeting with "Nancy Warren" who would continue to work inside the Pentagon and be one of his contacts in the Washington, D.C. area. She would continue communication with others who would become part of his Earth contacts.

There are still to this day many adversaries to human freedom. These parasites have imbedded themselves in all phases of human society and will never be exposed except by extraterrestrial intervention. There are confused individuals who have perfected a saucer-type aircraft. Some of these are the result of an attempt by some to institute a master race. Remnants of this group still exist. These craft which they designed are still seen from time to time in areas of South America where some of those involved in the original plans still reside. These should not be confused with the spacecraft originating from other worlds or those coming from the interior of this planet. Nor should the occupants of craft originating from other worlds be confused with those "evil messengers" who do not originate from Earth but were cast INTO it after the first "war" ever recorded. They are in league with Earthly lowgrades who have condemned themselves because of their own choices.

The Spaceman Departs

On March 16, Val dematerialized and departed from this phase of his Earthly mission. His next stop was the outskirts of Alexandria, Virginia where his ship and his crew awaited his arrival, hidden by a wooded area. It was no problem for him to reassemble the atoms of his body inside his ship.

As his craft rose slowly, a number of people stopped and pointed excitedly in his direction. Others stood motionless, transfixed by the sight which they beheld. He felt such a tremendous feeling of love for all of them. There was no panic in them...just curiosity and a strong desire to know more. Then, as the USAF jets were scrambled, and with the force field now in full use, the planes darted past the ship unable to see them now. Even ground radar lost them on their equipment. Confusion once again reigned.

On the way back to Victor One, he meditated on his home planet, the low, heavy, colorful clouds, the even temperatures, the perfectly diffused sunlight that made shadows almost nonexistent, the lushness of the rich green grass surrounding his home. He was informed of several Earth people with whom he would maintain contact for a long time into the future. Strangely enough, those who knew of his presence, yet who claimed disbelief, were those who feared the most. Others figured THEY should have been the ones contacted and not those who were.

Upon returning to his home planet, he advised the Council of Central Control of the results of his Earth visit

including the failure of the leaders of the United States to "take him up" on his offer of advice and assistance to the human family. He was given the following instructions:
1. To mingle with and become as Earth people
2. To work and labor in Earth enterprises
3. To help those who encounter possible threat or danger while striving for world peace
4. To give them advice and guidance
5. To entrust with superior knowledge those who have proven themselves
6. Divulge the essence of their mission to the collective national leaders of Earth, *only when the time is right.*

As of this writing, he continues with this mission, at the same time assisting in preventing our "civilization" from being the cause of orbital chaos by the destruction of our planet.

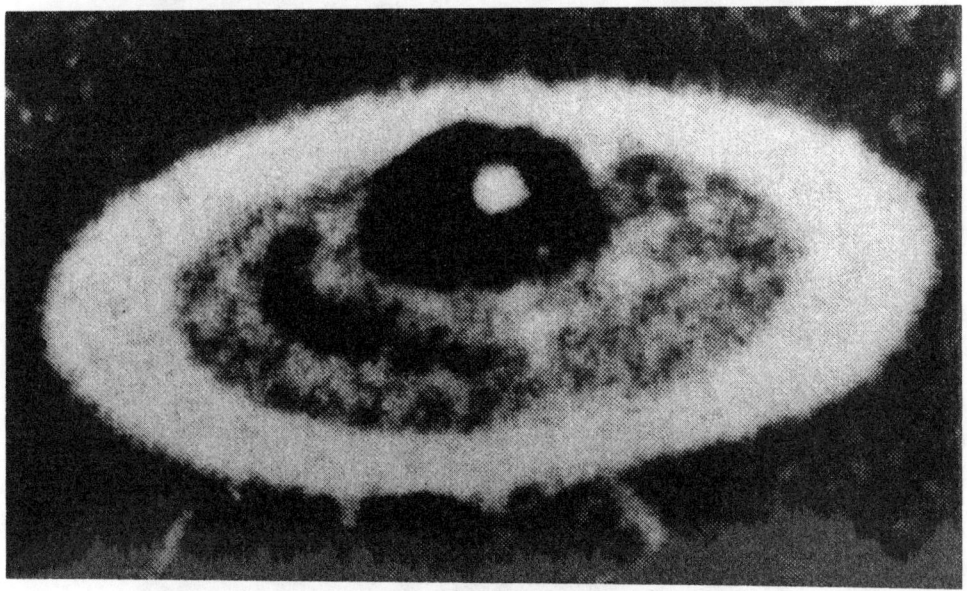

Flying disc over South Africa.

Stranger At The Pentagon

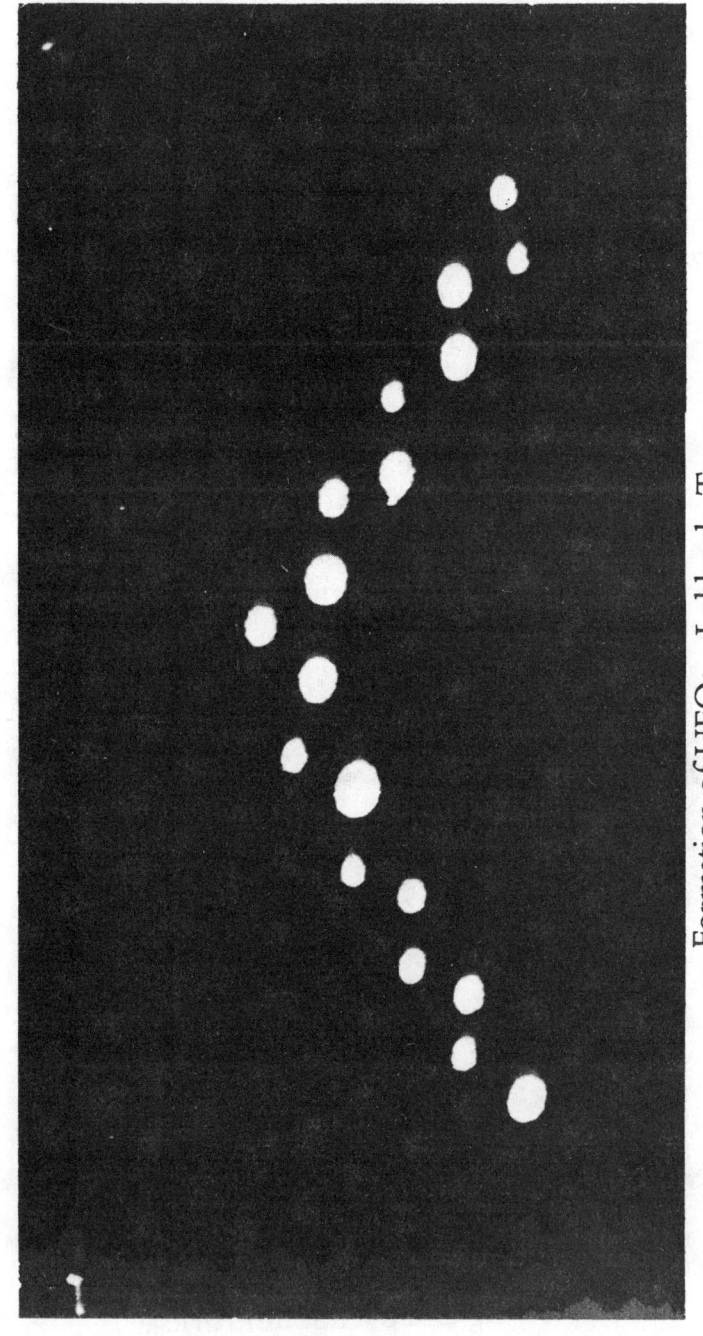

Formation of UFOs—Lubbock, Texas.

Chapter Two
The Meetings Begin

Having left the Pentagon with energy, enthusiasm and more questions, I looked forward to the next meeting with this unusual visitor from another planet. It would be approximately one year later before I would hear his voice and see his face again. During that period of time, I had been questioned by the F.B.I. regarding my strange adventure of entering the Pentagon. In fact, they met me at my flight into New York upon my return from the Washington, D.C. meetings I had been conducting.

I was taken to the F.B.I. office where I was interrogated for nearly three hours. I myself could hardly believe the experience I had just had, let alone attempting to convince government intelligence officers the same. They finally gave me a polygraph test and I was allowed to leave.

Riding the subway to my parents home that afternoon, I had time to ponder the events of the previous days. I continued to wonder exactly what Val had meant when he said to me the words "when the time is right". I still had no idea when or if I would ever meet him again. Meanwhile, I tried to convince my family that I was still sane.

Second Meeting

It wasn't until nearly one year later that I was driving in Beverly Hills, California, when Val suddenly appeared in the back seat of my car. To say I was startled would be quite an understatement. I stopped the car and he got into the passenger seat in front and our second meeting began.

"Hello, Frank. How are you?", he said again.

I was right back at the Pentagon wondering what would happen next. His warm smile and his friendly manner at once

Daytime shot by Paul Villa.

Convention location: Mainz, West Germany

set me at ease and he continued the conversation by asking me questions about my work, my family, etc. Meetings such as this would continue for the next several years. I would be driving along and there he would be...standing on a street corner, crossing the street in front of my car. Surprisingly, these meetings were more of the "get acquainted" type. My getting acquainted with him, of course.

As the years went on, he began to confide certain information to me regarding some of their activities on this planet. He informed me that they were in the process of establishing what he called "communication bases" in private residences. From city to city, in major areas around the globe, individuals of high character and committment had been contacted and their assistance had been enlisted to accomplish this goal. Today, some of these areas include Reno, Nevada; San Diego, California; Geneva, Switzerland; and even Los Angeles, California.

In these homes you will find communication equipment unlike any you can scarcely imagine. There is a holographic communicator which operates in the middle of the room. All you have to do is sit in a chair located along the perimeter and suddenly you are seeing the physical image of the one to whom you are speaking. Perhaps this is what is meant by "personal contact".

The first time I saw this device in use, at a home in the Los Angeles area, I could hardly believe my eyes. Actually, I went up to the image and ran my hand through it. It looked so true to life, as if the person were actually standing right in front of me. That person got quite a laugh out of my bold, unusual actions.

In addition to this holographic device, there is other equipment with which those space visitors can communicate with other of their ships that are located on and around Earth including the Starship which is their "home base" and orbits above this planet.

In Our Midst

In order to blend with others on this planet, they use public transportation to move about from city to city. For the most part, this would be flying by commercial airlines. It is amazing to watch the faces and reactions of people when these Angelic beings come into the presence of Earthlings. Some will feel a strange sensation throughout their bodies, some will giggle and not know why, some will become very emotional, perhaps tears will well up in their eyes. Others still will be totally unaware that there is someone present who is not of this world.

When they are working in a particular city, a car is provided for them by their host in that city. There are others who contribute of their good fortune to assure that all the needs of Val and any of his crew are met in the process of appearing as normal as possible as they go about their work on this planet. While they have the capability to materialize anything that they wish, this action would obviously draw unnecessary attention to them and thereby defeat their purpose.

On rare occasions, when the need arises, they will use one of their smaller transport ships, such as the one which Val used to land in Alexandria, Virginia. Most times, this is at night and when time is of the essence.

Time continued to pass and as I became more acquainted with Val and others, he began to prepare me for yet another fantastic experience which would shortly take place, an experience I will never forget as long as I live.

Top-shaped ship photographed by Dan Fry in Oregon.

Chapter Three
A Life Spared

A knock at the door...a special delivery letter...an invitation to be a guest speaker at a UFO Convention in West Germany. This was to begin a chapter in my life that was designed by certain "dark forces" to remove me from circulation permanently.

The members of our party made their way to New York's Kennedy Airport in November, 1967. After our flight from Los Angeles, we had several hours before leaving for Frankfurt. I took time to phone my parents who resided in New York at that time.

Many thoughts were going through our minds as we discussed our itinerary which would take us to several European countries for the first time. We had been invited to West Germany, Finland, Sweden and England on this trip.

To our great surprise, when we boarded the plane, our seats had been given to a woman who was traveling with three children and required the bulkhead seats which had previously been assigned to us. We followed the steward as he led us to the first class seating.

With a smile, he said, "I hope that you have a pleasant trip."

We Arrive in Germany

With that, he winked and carried on with his own business. The flight had experienced some delay in departing from Kennedy Airport but our flight to Germany was uneventful and we landed in the cool overcast.

Evidently we had missed the party who was to meet us in Frankfort because of our delay. It was almost comical to call someone on the telephone because the coin rang up in the middle of our conversation at least three times and I found myself talking into a dead phone. However, we finally did make a good connection and were instructed to proceed to Mainz by taxi. Our driver's English was limited to three expressions..."yes", "no", and "forty marks". A comedy to be sure.

At last we arrived in Mainz and the taxi wandered through several narrow yet interesting streets which are typical in most European communities. He finally came to a stop in front of the Mainzerhoff Hotel, took our luggage and deposited it in the lobby and delivered us safe and sound to the German delegation who assisted us in registering at the front desk. I personally anticipated a very wonderful convention not realizing that this trip could have cost me my life.

Herr Karl Veit, the convention host and a dear friend, greeted us warmly as we entered the dining room on the top floor of the hotel. The windows overlooked the beautiful Rhine River. A number of boats floated by, reflecting the sun of that beautiful but chilly afternoon. Others, including Professor Herman Oberth (known as the father of rocketry) and Coleman Von Keviczky (who had publicly challenged the Pentagon on many occasions on UFOs), stood up at the table and made us feel welcome. Mr. Veit ordered dinner for all of us and we sat down to enjoy this festive occasion.

It was quite impossible to order even a simple glass of water with our meals in any country during our trip unless we called it by name. So consequently, that was the first phrase we learned in each country we visited. The only place this was not necessary was in England. At least they understood what we meant, although when you visit an English-speaking country after several other foreign-language countries, you almost feel as if you don't know your own language anymore. It was quite strange.

We were visiting these countries not to involve ourselves in any political discussions but to share our findings about unidentified flying objects and the possibility of life, as we know it, existing in the mass universe. We were cautioned not to participate in any political altercations.

The convention hall was within walking distance from the hotel and so the first morning most of us walked through the brisk cool air, glad we had brought warm clothing. The streets were exceedingly clean and the people very warm and friendly. The members of the press met us at the hall and following a brief session of questions and picture taking, we met other members of Mr. Veit's staff along with many other people who expressed their joy in meeting all of us.

The atmosphere was charged with excitement and expectancy. Flowers decorated the hall along with the flags of all nations. Many of the speakers had already arrived and were huddled here and there answering the questions of very curious people.

As the convention was officially opened by Mr. Veit, the speakers were introduced. They included Coleman Von Keviczky, Professor Herman Oberth, Dr. Wilk Martin, J.V. Jacobi, Professor Alfred Nahon, Karl L. Veit, Erfinder Friedrich Hummel, D. Grasso, W. Losensky Philet, Roberto Pinotti, Ing. Erich Halid, Dr. Kurt Kauffmann, Ing. Walter Ohr, Frau Luise Eschig, D.F. Ross, Professor Dr. G. Macaluso, Ewald Norr, Eric von Daniken and myself.

Frank E. Stranges, Ph.D.

A Deadly Experience

I was scheduled to appear twice. Once to present a UFO lecture and again to present our UFO documentary film, "Phenomena 7.7". The film was scheduled to be shown on the evening of November 5th at 16:00 hours. Prior to that time, I was called to be interviewed by two men from a large Italian newspaper-type magazine. One said he was a reporter and the other a photographer. We sat at a small table in the dining room during which time we had a light lunch. Most of their questions were aimed at learning the full facts regarding my contact with Val Thor. They said they had read my books, "My Friend From Beyond Earth", "Flying Saucerama" and "Stranger At The Pentagon". With their tape recorder going, they questioned me about as many details concerning Val as I could give them. I gave them a detailed account leading up to my meeting with Val. They kept asking me over and over again, "Where is he now?" I responded with the same answer each time and occasionally dipped my spoon into my bowl of tomato soup.

Then, a young man tapped me on the shoulder and informed me that there was a long-distance call for me from Finland. I excused myself from the table and proceeded to take the call. It was from Reverend Leo Meller, one of the sponsoring pastors of the Full Gospel Businessmen's Association, who along with the Methodist Church, sponsored us at the University of Helsinki. Reverend Meller called to inquire as to what time we were expecting to arrive in Helsinki. Following the phone conversation, I returned to the table only to learn that the two men were gone. The table had been wiped clean except for my bowl of soup.

Perplexed, I sat down and swallowed a tablespoon full of the soup and then I knew something was wrong...very wrong. I tasted a gritty substance that burned like fire all the way down into my stomach. I made a quick grab for a glass of water on a nearby counter. I immediately located my interpreter, Mr. Anthony Low, and together we rushed back to the hotel. By this time, blood was trickling out of my mouth and down the front of my shirt. He knew I was growing sicker and weaker with each passing moment.

A Strange Mixture

Upon reaching my room, he quickly administered a dose of powder which he stirred into a glass of water and which he had mixed before leaving the University where he was studying. As a medical student, he had access to medical supplies. He did not tell me the contents of the vial because HE DID NOT KNOW. He claimed he was "instructed" to mix this substance and bring it with him to Mainz.

I swallowed the contents of the glass and fell into a deep sleep. Yet I was keenly aware that I was not alone in this experience. Upon awakening, the pain and discomfort had vanished. I reached for a glass of water which was on the night stand and slowly sipped some. It felt good and cool, all the way down into my stomach.

Within a matter of moments, the telephone rang. It was Val Thor calling from Switzerland. His words sounded very mellow yet stern.

He said, "Frank, how many times have I cautioned you to be very careful with whom you meet?"

He continued, "There are many, many lessons to be learned and oftimes, they are painful. However, I am certain that you gained from this experience. Please exercise extreme care."

Val stated that there were, in fact, men in black, not just in dress but in motive and in heart. He said he would elaborate later when we could meet in person in the United States. He also added that several of his people would be watching us for the duration of our European trip.

Forces of Darkness

Following a "cleansing" of my system, I felt like a new born babe. Conversations that I had enjoyed with Val in the past were streaming into my thinking. He made mention at one time that not all space beings were of God, that there were some motivated by the forces of darkness and that additional information would be given to me at a later time. I was then to learn the meaning of those words. That in the beginning when there was war in the heavenlies, Lucifer and his "crew" had been cast down into the Earth. The only power they lost was that of being in the presence of the Divine Creator. And Lucifer was still permitted to travel through a small corridor into the presence of God where to this day he attempts to accuse the saints. Val informed me of many things regarding these "angels". He told me that it is important for all men and women who are children of True Light to learn the art of Spiritual as well as mental self-defense.

When I returned to the convention hall, all was ready for my presentation. The audience response was warm and friendly as they listened with interest, desirous to learn the

Stranger At The Pentagon

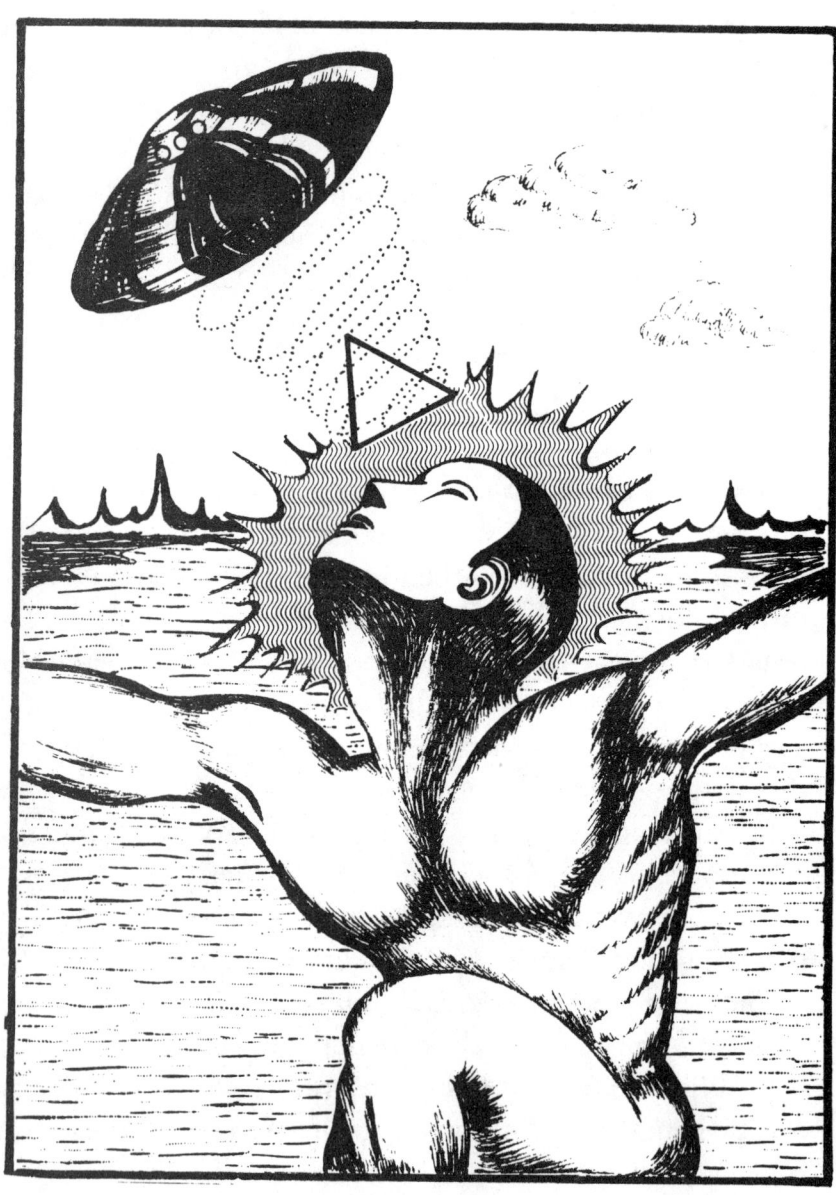

truth about space, science and true religion.

The following day, inquiry was made and we were not too amazed to learn that the Italian magazine had no knowledge of the two who claimed to represent them at the convention.

Many years ago, I gave my life over to Jesus Christ and I knew that in years to come, many revelations would be given me for the purpose of showing the Way to others. However, the Way would not be easy...but then again, it would be fruitful because of the fact that there are many blessings for those who dare to walk "out of step" from the rest of the crowd as one's ears become attuned to the beat of the "distant drummer".

Another experience, another warning, another time to prove that God is with us and that there is help available to those who dare to believe. However, the best was still to come.

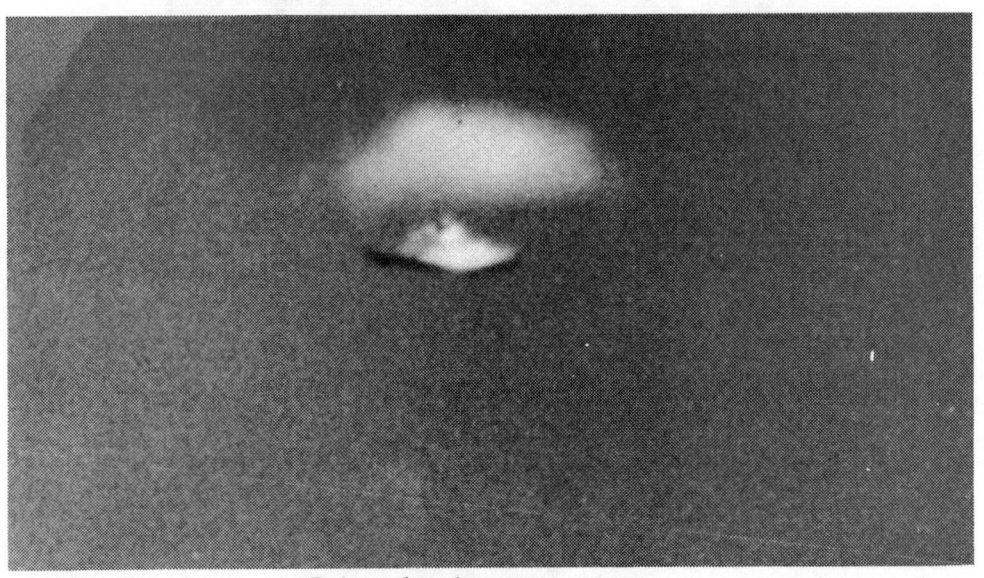

Painted Lake, Wisconsin.

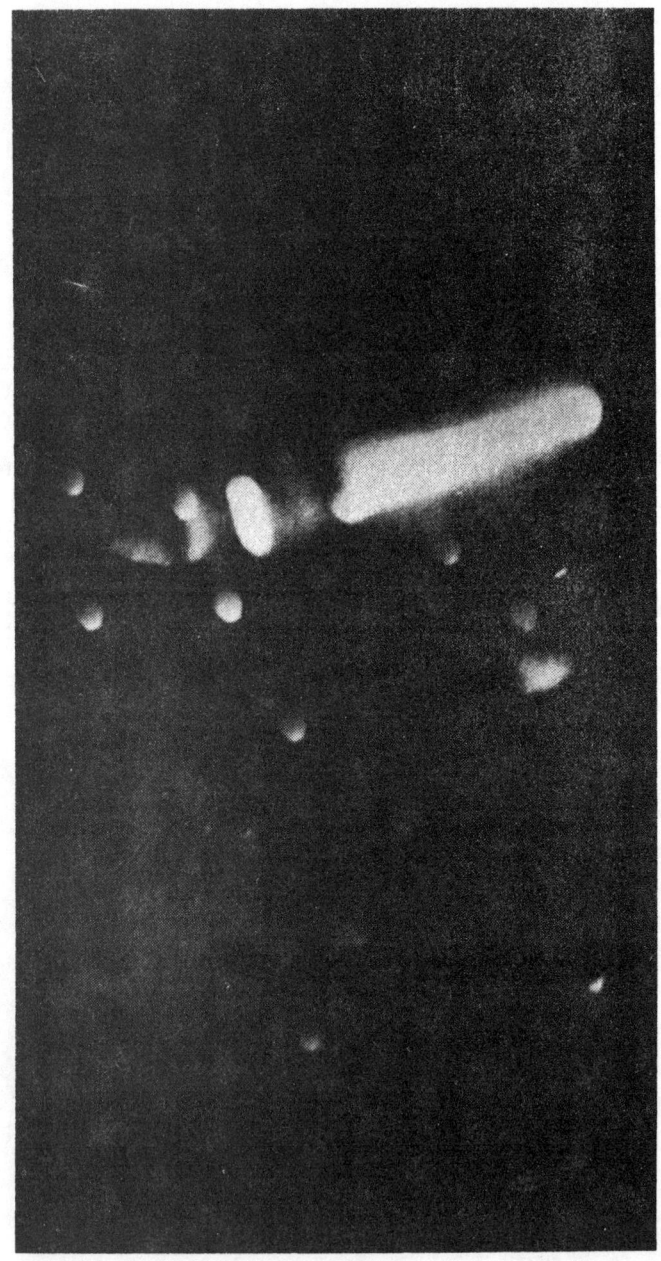

Bright cigar above Japan.

Chapter Four
Welcome Aboard

Paris, France.

Frank E. Stranges, Ph.D.

June 5, 1968, will go down in history as a day when many were born, successful business deals were signed and sealed, some may even have lost their shirts on a deal gone sour. It will be remembered as the date of a beautiful wedding. a testimonial dinner, a divorce, an accident and perhaps even a black spot for the family, the loss of a loved one...a father, brother, mother sister, son or daughter, or a government official. Namely, the death of Robert Kennedy. A case of lack of security, a lack of caution, a disregard of a solemn warning. I cannot give a detailed account of what actually took place that fateful day at the Ambassador Hotel in Los Angeles, but suffice it to say that the authorities who were in charge of the investigation know more than what was admitted to the press. Reports have surfaced in recent years regarding the removal of certain pieces of door and frame in the immediate area. Crucial pieces of evidence have come up missing.

But let us go back to that morning. A phone call, an airplane flight to San Diego, California. I was contacted by Val who instructed me to meet him at the San Diego Airport. He ushered me to the parking lot where we got into his car and drove toward the Mexican border. Little did I realize that this particular trip was to be one of many that would increase my understanding of this one called Val Thor and his mission to this planet.

During the drive to the border, we discussed a few items of interest. He made it a point to call out the names of various of my closest associates who were involved in helping me to spread the truth in every corner possible.

We pulled up to the border crossing, were greeted by the

border guards on either side of the car, then proceeded to drive south for many miles to a small town called San Felipe, Sonora, Mexico. Few people were walking the dusty streets. A few American tourists were making their way toward the restaurant that featured seafood. San Felipe is a coastal town almost surrounded by water. It is a very quiet place to come for a rest...and perhaps some fishing.

However, we were not there for any of those reasons. Val parked the car in the parking area directly behind the restaurant. Then we started to climb over a few rocks and found ourselves walking along the beach, out of sight from the restaurant. The small shacks that housed the townspeople could not be seen from where we were walking. We boarded a small boat, started the engine and began our ride. I still did not know where we were going.

UFO on the Water

Then I saw it. An actual, saucer-shaped vehicle was sitting on the water. I noticed a strange phenomena. The waves were gently rocking a power boat tied to the rough mooring, causing the boat to rise and fall. However, I noticed that the space craft DID NOT MOVE. I was to be informed later that the ship was equipped with a pencil-fine beam that when fixed on any solid object kept the ship from moving even one degree from that fixed position. As we neared the ship, it glistened in the light of the sun that was beautifully setting, rapidly. We sailed close to the craft with the motor cut off. Then an aperture opened, revealing two smiling faces. One man and one woman greeted me by name, took my hand, lifted me into the ship and then reached down for Val. A short time later, the small power-craft was also raised aboard and stowed in a compartment where a much larger power craft was also seen.

My first impression was one of great exhilaration mingled with joy and excitement. I had read from time to time true accounts that had changed the lives of other UFO researchers and investigators. I have read many books that carefully outlined the experiences of those who had experienced actual space contact. But now it was different. It was happening to me. I remembered how my colleagues in the Christian ministry looked with disdain upon anyone who would dare relate incidents about "space people", "space vehicles" and such. But now I found myself caring less what anyone would possibly think of me because of my own experiences. I was there!!!

Purifying Sensation

I was ushered by these wonderful people to a room where I was requested to completely disrobe. I did so without question. I then walked through a compartment that resembled a shower... only without the water. I felt a purifying sensation all over my body. I no longer required my eyeglasses to see. This is another phenomena on board the ship that was quite "unscientific". I felt extremely good in body, soul and spirit.

After walking through the "shower compartment" I was issued a white outfit that resembled what we would call "overalls". The fabric was lightweight just as Val's garment had been when he showed it to me at the Pentagon. However it was a different fabric than his. Their "boots" were tight

Stranger At The Pentagon

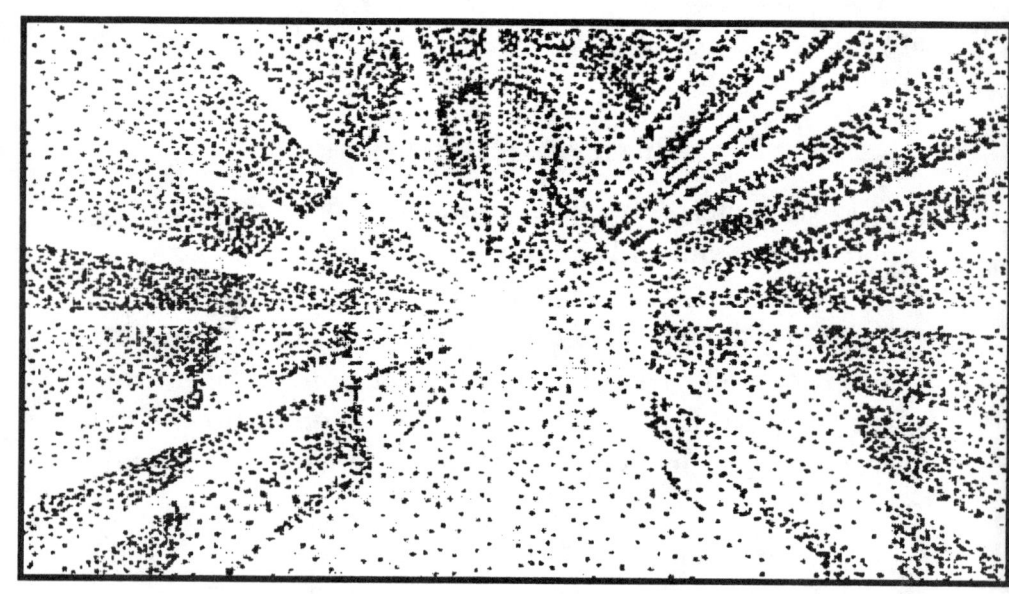

The fire of God touches Val.

fitting while mine were loose.

I was then directed toward the door and was accompanied by a lovely woman called "Teel" to Val's quarters. During my several hours aboard the craft, I was to encounter many wonders that were so scientifically simple that I could hardly believe it.

There were a series of buttons on the wall and Val pushed one of them. Suddenly one section of the wall became transparent and the scene outside was in full view. This occurrence would happen many times again, even when we would be traveling in one of his small craft. This was quite unnerving at first because your mind simply does not have any point of reference for this type of experience. It took a long time for me to get used to this. In fact, it still amazes me to such an extent that I don't think I will ever be used to it.

Kennedy Assassination

Val's compartment was quite spacious, comfortable and done in a light color decor with a master viewscreen at eye level. Making me comfortable, he started to give me an insight into phases of my UFO investigation that I had never explored personally. This information, on such subjects as the hollow Earth theory, the black hole mystery, the Bermuda triangle, etc., would be revealed in my later writings and audio recordings. He also informed me that Bobby Kennedy and he had met in the Los Angeles area shortly after I delivered Mr. Kennedy's letter to Val. He informed me that his first impression of Mr. Kennedy was that he was a very nervous and suspicious man, but that he was also a man who should not be crossed, politically. Val went on to relate just a brief report of his meeting. However, he did point out that he did not believe that Bobby was going to heed his advice. A look of sorrow came over Val's face. I had never seen this expression before. As the evening wore on, we had assembled in a large room where the viewscope had tuned in to a certain hotel, The Ambassador, in Los Angeles, California. There was much commotion, excitement and confusion in the scene. There were approximately fifty-five "crew" present for the viewing. I was made to understand that the same scene was being transmitted throughout the ship for all to see and hear the tragic event that was to occur.

Val stated that he had been queried by Mr. Kennedy as to his chances for the Presidency to which Val had replied, "Mr. Kennedy, four years from now, you would stand an excellent chance of winning. But, I beg you to remain far away from the political race this year."

This, he repeated to him several times. Val was very concerned and so were the members of his immediate staff. Tension grew as we saw Mr. Kennedy walking, pressing through the crowd.

Val then said, "God, help him."

Suddenly, several shots rang out and it appeared that all hell had cut loose. Val did not move from his seat.

Teel jumped up and said, "If only he had listened!"

Many of his followers, including Rosey Grier, attempted to shield the body of Mr. Kennedy from further abuse, but it was too late. Shots rang out again and in the confusion, one bullet found its mark. Mr. Kennedy was down on the floor while many shouted and screamed and still others began to attack Sirhan Sirhan.

The investigation that ensued was similar to that of the late President of the United States, John F. Kennedy, and was covered up in like manner. Someday, the entire truth may come out. Val and the group watched with grave concern. Following the removal of Mr. Kennedy from the hotel, the set was turned off in Val's quarters.

He looked directly at me and said, "Frank, it is impossible to go through life without maintaining the covering of the protection of Almighty God. We are protected by His Divine Power while you, Frank, must depend upon the help and protection of His Son, Jesus Christ. You see, Frank, it is not only important but also necessary to your own Spiritual well-being to contain this protection every day of your own life. You have an important mission to accomplish on this planet and you will come against the very powers of Lucifer himself because you pose a direct threat to his kingdom. Practice the presence of Christ and walk in His Divine Presence. We will do what we can to help you but you must be the one to make the decisions. If you make a wrong or erroneous decision, learn by that mistake and then go on into the perfection that your Lord Jesus Christ has foreordained for you and others that will set you apart from and above those who are involved in the works of darkness."

An Alien Dinner

With that, we went to an area where several members of the crew were eating and drinking. I was able to enjoy food and drink that did not originate on this planet. The food was of high protein value and the drink, green in color, tasted very similar to papaya. It was very refreshing. Val informed me that from time to time, I would be invited to return to the ship in order to cleanse my system and to take part in discussions with others regarding world affairs.

Following that brief session, I was given a guided tour of the ship by Val and Teel. It was interesting to note that there were no square corners on the ship whatever. The one area that fascinated me most was the auditorium. It was here that the crew was briefed each day, but only after the morning worship service. They worship the same God as I and recognize Christ as being the Son of God who came to this planet Earth for the purpose of winning the human family back to the Eternal Father. Val said in one of his talks that God was no respector of persons and would reveal His eternal Truths to whom would receive them.

Advanced "Technology"

Later I was shown to my own guest quarters which were quite unique. Again, no square corners. The color was pale blue made even softer by the indirect lighting which appeared to come from the ceiling. Walking across the floor was like standing in the thickest, puffiest clouds you can imagine. It seemed to "fit" the form of your foot as you walked. The room actually looked quite bare when you first walked in. Everything to serve your needs was located in the wall and with the push of a button, it was at your service. The bed, the desk, all at your fingertips. A viewscreen was visible in the wall at eye level as you sat in the chair provided for your complete comfort.

One amusing incident occurred when the needs of nature had to be attended. I went into the bathroom and was embarrassed to note the obvious absence of toilet tissue. Then it happened. I heard a voice within my mind which I immediately recognized as belonging to Val.

He said, "Frank, look to your right. You will find three buttons. Push the first, then the second and then the third, in that order."

I could hear Teel's laugh as I proceeded to press the first button. The sensation was that of a rapid warm wind similar to a jet of air, blowing beneath the seat. The process entirely crystalized the waste matters and caused it to drop from me. Then the second button was another jet blast of a different pressure and temperature. Finally, the third button. This produced a pleasant, fragrant substance that made me feel as though I had been washed, cleaned, powdered and perfumed.

As I came out of the bathroom, no one paid any attention to me although I had a strong feeling that everybody in the room knew what had happened.

Suddenly Teel broke the silence by saying, "Well, do you want to take one home with you?"

A few of them laughed and went on about their business.

After meeting privately with Val, I proceeded to sleep for a few hours and in the morning, Val drove me back to San Diego where I again boarded a plane, this time bound for Los Angeles. I pondered the events which had taken place during the past day. My heart skipped a beat as the thrill of the blessings I had been chosen to receive began to register in my mind. And sadness continued to overshadow my soul as I recalled witnessing the life of Robert Kennedy snuffed out in an instant.

I now knew without question that the time was here to

begin letting the world know that truly we are not alone in the universe and that God did not confine His acts of creating life as we know it to this, the third planet from the Sun.

George Stockton took this shot in N.J.

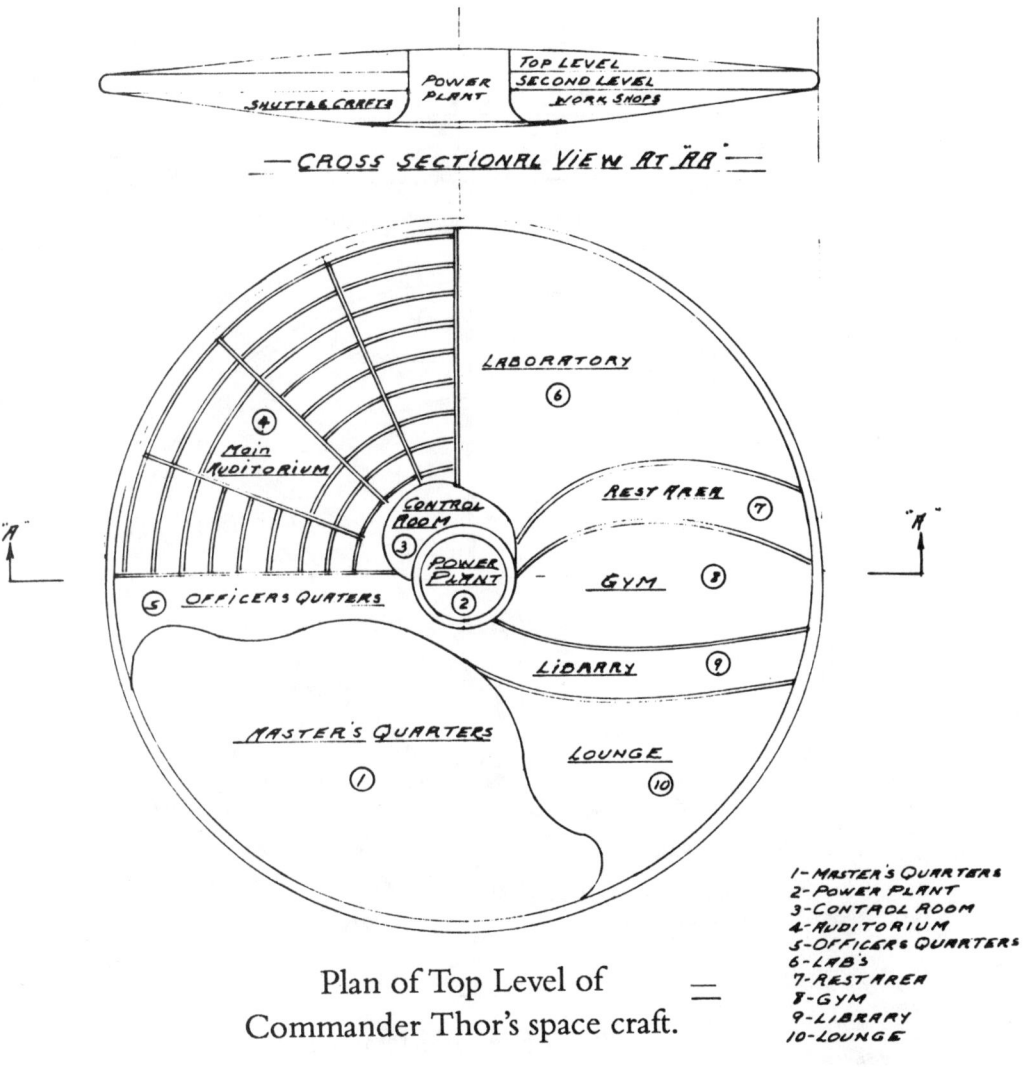

Plan of Top Level of Commander Thor's space craft.

Drawn By — J. B. La Voie

Stranger At The Pentagon

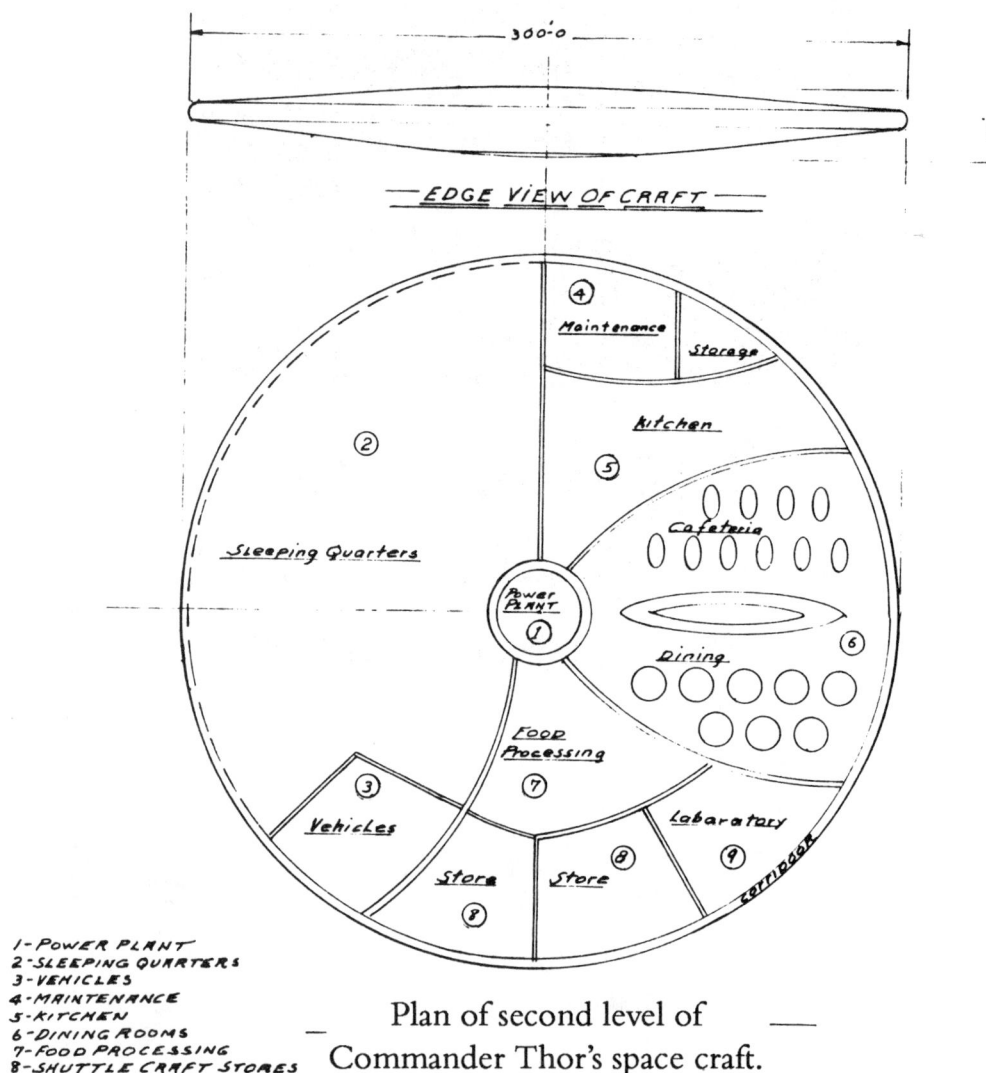

1 - POWER PLANT
2 - SLEEPING QUARTERS
3 - VEHICLES
4 - MAINTENANCE
5 - KITCHEN
6 - DINING ROOMS
7 - FOOD PROCESSING
8 - SHUTTLE CRAFT STORES
9 - LAB

Plan of second level of Commander Thor's space craft.

Chapter Five
Val's Appointment to Commander

A very long time ago, Commander Val was an instructor (at what we would consider a University level) on Venus. Bear in mind that he is one of those beings who was directly created by the Hand of Almighty God Himself. There are times when one such as Val will elect to attach himself to parents of other children, usually because there is a kinship of thoughts and ideas that together they can perpetuate the Glory of Almighty God throughout the universe. Therefore, Val is considered one who was created by The Father, yet NOT in as high a position as Jesus Christ because Jesus Christ came to Earth as the very EMBODIMENT OF THE CREATOR OF CREATORS.

Val is in a special class by himself. Yet, because of a desire to be a part of a special Venusian family, he has also taken upon himself the pleasure of having a ready-made family; namely, Donn, Thonn and Doc. These are all fellow members of the THOR family. In the beginning, Val was called VALIANT. After attaching himself to the family, he then adopted their name THOR.

The Land of Quello

Following the creation of the Earth, there was a period of time during which The Creator brought into existence several other creations. One of the most popular was the creation of the land and people of QUELLO. This was a marvelous creation accompanied by many, many developments that attested to the creativity and imagination of man. But, as the story goes, this awesome power went to their heads and they immediately, with the help of "Lucifer", placed themselves in a self-destruct position. They defied all of the perfect laws of God, violated His Perfect Will as well as the laws governing their own society. Consequently, they were banished from the face of the Earth. Almighty God then proceeded to create another man on the surface of this planet.

Commander Val bore witness to these amazing events and volunteered to observe the Earth in order to gain a closer look at what was transpiring there. However, much time passed before Commander Val was permitted to personally visit Earth.

He continued to advance and soon became an instructor. Teaching the young people the mysteries of the universe gave him great joy, yet he still longed for something more.

When he was a younger man, Val was performing what would be considered to be menial tasks that to him were not too important. He prayed and meditated for many days without ceasing. Although he felt within himself that someday he would be a Starship Commander, he grew impatient.

One day, while walking along the shores of one of the most beautiful bodies of water within the confines of Venus, an amazing yet wonderful event took place that was to change his life forever and fulfill his fondest dream.

Ring of Fire

Suddenly, without warning, from out of the crystal lake, a finger of fire rose from the waters thus revealing the hand and then a full-length arm. It was pointed directly at Val. He remained motionless as the fifiery finger touched his lips.

He heard what he describes as a Majestic Voice saying to him, "Valiant, you have been created for a Divine purpose. Your lips will speak words of wisdom, understanding and knowledge to people on a far-away planet. Let your heart be filled with the expectation that very soon you will be sent to accomplish the most important task for which you have been prepared."

Commander Val told me that he then felt the power of Almighty God not only flooding his soul, but cloaking him with supernatural power that originated from The Father. Within days, he met face-to-face with Jesus Christ. This took place during a special time of worship and praise that raised the consciousness of the people to a much higher level than ever before. A FLAME OF FIRE filled the temple and small tongues of FIRE sat upon everyone in attendance. The Master summoned Val to the platform. A special robe of power and authority was placed around his shoulders. The flame of fire continued to rest upon his head. The Master placed His Divine Hand upon Val's head and a blessing was pronounced upon him. The power of The Almighty was so great that many witnessing the sight fell to the floor in adoration. Val's mission was completely spelled out to him before many thousands of witnesses Then Val knew that the task of bringing light to the planet Earth was inevitable.

While The Master concluded the ceremony, Val was instructed to remain on the platform. The Master placed His Divine Arms around Val and charged him with the task that lay before him.

Within a brief time, The Master announced a special RING OF FIRE ceremony that was to be performed by Val and others BEFORE they would set foot on the planet Earth. This RING OF FIRE would protect him and all the others permitted to serve with him. Their mission was under the

DIRECT guidance of the Lord Jesus Christ and remains so to this day.

Appointed Commander

Following this experience, Val accepted the appointment as Commander and the assignment to travel to Earth to do all within his power to carry out the Divine instructions and establish bases on Earth in order to implement the aims and purposes of his appointment. To this day, Val travels back and forth to Venus and is still in command of the Venusians who have been assigned to this planet.

It was only a few short years ago that he felt the time had become right to share this RING OF FIRE ceremony and prayers with the members of our association. (Please see Chapter Seven)

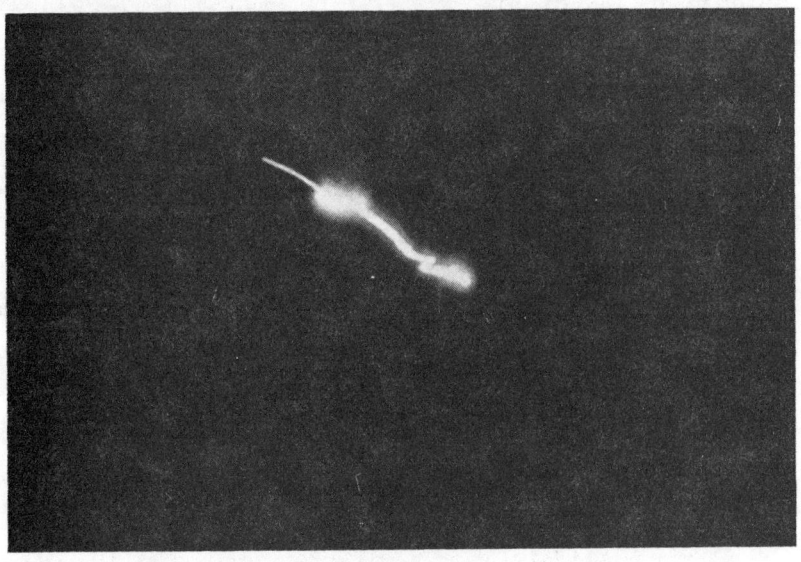

Photo by Bob Strong, Warminster, England.

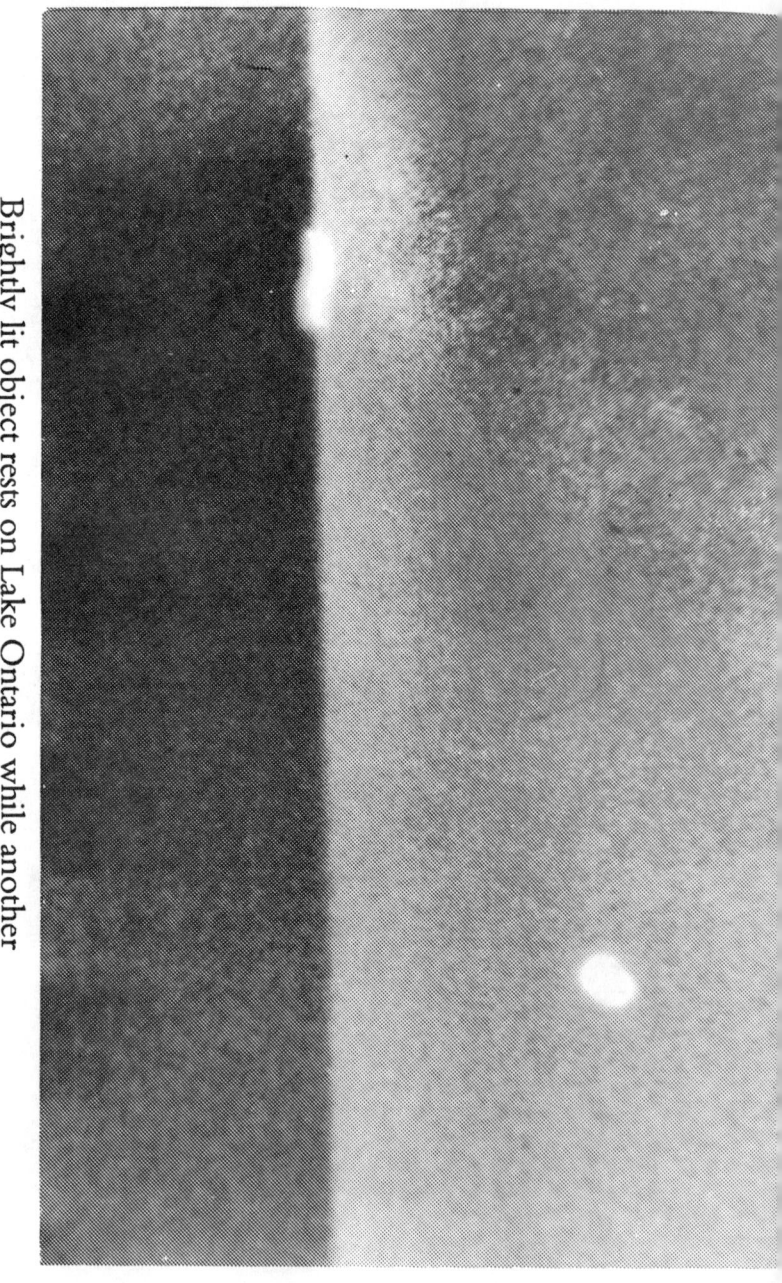

Brightly lit object rests on Lake Ontario while another UFO shoots across the sky.

Chapter Six
The Airport Attack

As a researcher and investigator of Unidentified Flying Objects, I have been swamped with information coming from various parts of the world regarding a phase of UFO research that is avoided by many. That phase involves a certain group called "men in black". A number of researchers over the years have met with unusual accidents while investigating UFO accounts. Several have even met with untimely death under mysterious circumstances. We cannot afford to ignore the fact that there are forces of darkness surrounding this planet.

I have encountered many obstacles during my research that would tend to discourage me rather than encourage me. This is but one of the aspects of UFO research about which Val taught me.

The Men in Black

One afternoon in January, 1974, I was summoned for a meeting with Val and several of his people on the outskirts of Las Vegas, Nevada. The Sun had started to descend behind the mountains as my plane taxied to the ramp. I noticed the unhappy faces of those who had left their "donations" to the welfare of Las Vegas. I noticed two young men, attired in tight-fitting black outfits waving to me. Calling me by name, I thought them to be friends of Val. One of them took my briefcase and I was instructed to follow them to a black Cadillac parked at the curb. Another man, also dressed in black, was sitting behind the wheel. This did not strike me as odd because many limousine drivers wear similar uniforms.

I was invited to sit in the rear by one of the men who had already climbed into the back seat. The second man sat on the right of me. The smell of cigars should have tipped me off. However, the excitement of seeing Val again superseded my caution. Space people DO NOT SMOKE and are NEVER around people who do. I should have known then that something was radically wrong.

An uneasy feeling came over me as the Cadillac pulled away from the curb. I saw red lights and heard warning bells inside my head. There was no further conversation until we pulled over to the side of the road several blocks away from the airport.

The gentlemen to my right said, "Get out."

He proceeded to exit the car and my heart was pounding at such a rapid rate that I thought it would burst. As I stooped to get out of the car, the man behind me must have braced himself against the side of the door and planted his feet with a firm shove directly against my kidneys. I was sent sprawling to the desert floor, face full of sand, and immediately pounced upon by the duo.

Calling Upon the Lord

I remembered some of my martial arts study and quickly rolled out of their way for a few seconds and sprang to my feet. It was then that I struck back at them, at the same time calling on the name of the Lord Jesus Christ.

Many "passive" Christians who read this narrative will most likely be horrified when they learn that I dared to lift my hand in self protection. I defended myself to the best of my ability. Again, I was thrown to the ground and kicked over and over again. My glasses were smashed but I could see well enough to get back on my feet and land a direct hit in the face of one of my attackers. I heard the crunch of broken cartilage while at the same time noticing that my hand was a bloody mess.

Meanwhile, the driver came rushing to the scene and plowed into the thick of battle. I caught him in the stomach with my right foot while lashing out again at the other two. Suddenly, a white Cadillac pulled in front of where the black one was parked. Two men rushed to my aid and I knew without any necessary introductions that these were the men whom I was supposed to have met at the Airport. Cars continued to pass by, some slowing down to look and continuing on their way.

The two men in silvery outfits attacked the trio to the point that they were immediately subdued. Without warning, the driver of the black Cadillac ran to his car and jumped behind the wheel. With his arm outstretched, Donn, one of the men from Val's spacecraft, melted the two rear tires. This vehicle was not going anywhere now. Donn then proceeded to "reach through the glass", without breaking it, and pull the driver through the window throwing him back on the ground with the other two.

I was instructed to get into the white Cadillac and I quickly obeyed. My two rescuers also got in but not before one of them "reached" into the trunk of the black Cad to remove my briefcase...without using a key. We proceeded a short distance.

Donn stopped our car, got out and slowly walked to the rear. He gestured with both hands toward the black car and within a matter of seconds, the car and the three men who were prostrate on the desert floor utterly vanished. There was no trace of the occurrence except for the disturbed sand and the rubber that had melted and "run like water".

Upon returning to the car, Donn anticipated my question of their new whereabouts.

Displaced

He replied, "Frank, let's just say that they are now displaced."

The car started again and we proceeded toward Henderson, Nevada. The conversation and atmosphere inside the car were enlightening to put it mildly. My companion in the back seat I was to learn later was Thonn, the brother of Donn, who is, in turn, Val Thor's brother.

We had a pleasant conversation, even though my right hand was still bleeding and the rest of my body felt like I had been struck by a Mack truck. Thonn reached into his pocket and showed me my wallet that had fallen out during the encounter. Also, he was holding the bent frame of my eyeglasses and said that when we arrived at the ship, they would be repaired. He placed his hand on my head and prayed for me that the healing power of God would work in my nervous system.

Force Field

Before long, we approached the entrance of the ship which was the only visible evidence of the presence of this 300-foot diameter vehicle which measures approximately three stories high. The force field rendered the bulk of the ship invisible.

The car came to a stop as we got out at the section of a

ramp where six other cars were parked. Val was on hand to welcome me aboard. With his arms around me, he made me feel as though I were home with my own people. The deep concern for my well-being was reflected on his face. I was taken to an area where I was to change clothes, shower and go on to the medical section. It was a familiar sight because of prior visits which I was obligated to undergo to detoxify my physical body. During the preparation, I was again warmly greeted by members of the crew, both men and women. These beautiful people literally reflected the Glory of The Creator of the universe.

Medical Center

The medical center is used for the benefit of people of Earth who visit Val's ship. Space people do not get sick or hurt on the job, nor do they become physically limited in any way, shape, manner or form. The medical facilities are comprised of the following:

An examination table (which also serves as an operating table) is made of a warm, soft, plastic-like substance (unlike the cold, metallic tables attested to by victims of kidnappings and abductions). There is a very powerful laser-type sun gun which is affixed to the ceiling. The soft pastel colors of the chamber lend themselves to peace and serenity. There is also soft music playing that certainly calms the nerves. All of the equipment tables, supplies, surgical instruments, etc. come out from the wall. When you first enter the chamber, all that you see is the table. The indirect lighting also lends itself to the tranquility of the room.

When it becomes necessary to draw blood (ours), it is

performed painlessly, without invading one's veins with a harsh needle. The small instrument that is used looks like a short transparent tube. When it is affixed to your arm, you hear the sound of a slight wind, no pain whatsoever. By the time the instrument is removed from your arm, the opening in your skin has healed WITH NO AFTER AFFECTS.

This treatment center is a real eye-opener. Of course, the medicines that are employed are all of a natural origin. No drugs of any kind are ever used. The chamber examining table is in the center of the room and actually form-fits to the contours of your body as you prepare for treatment. Every time you move, the table top adjusts to your body. If someone near the table were to put their hands next to you, the table would adjust itself to the pressure and the size of the hands.

The "read out" equipment is amazing. It comes out of the wall and passes over your body from head to toe and then back again. There are a series of lights and graphs that appear on the panel which has come into full view the moment the "read out" moves out from the wall.

The equipment scans your body and the panel reveals all of the physical disorders in it. This is quickly read and diagnosed by the "doctor" and the remedy is then quickly discussed and performed.

Healed by the Bluebeard

As I lay atop the soft white table, I was conscious of the beam of soft blue light that emitted from the cone-shaped instrument as it began to scan my bruised and battered body. I immediately went off into a deep sleep as the treatment process was completed.

Upon awakening, I felt good all over. Val was standing by while I dressed in my white outfit which was now made specifically for me by the on-board computer system and which included slippers. I was taken to Val's quarters where I was briefed on world conditions as well as world personalities. We discussed topics such as the role of the United Nations in world affairs, the coming gasoline crisis (which was really a man-made scheme to successfully escalate the price of gasoline), the role that Mr. Richard Nixon would be forced to play if he did not heed the constant warnings that he was receiving from friends from outer space, and a number of other subjects directly relating to my own personal activities.

Val went on to review the scope of faithfulness of those members of our organization whose hearts were with the overall goals of the program to help other members of the human family find Truth.

I received a personal discourse about the need for personal protection for myself and other members of our association. He informed me that "men in black" were no laughing matter and that it would behoove every honest UFO researcher and investigator to be warned that the M.I.B.'s were in the business of destroying and discrediting good on the face of this planet. Their threat is truly real.

Chapter Seven
The Ring of Fire

Closeup profile of Val Thor.

The date was April 11, 1985. My wife, Julie, and myself were traveling down Boulder Highway returning from a visit to Hoover Dam. The divided roadway was fairly busy that early afternoon when suddenly it happened.

"Watch out!" screamed my wife as the car seemed to appear from nowhere.

I quickly hit the brakes, swerved to avoid the blue car and was struck from behind by the automobile directly in back of us. This sent us racing into the dirt median area where we spun several times before finally coming to a complete stop. The dust had been so thick that we could not see out the windshield while spinning like a top. The impact had been so great that Julie's sunglasses were now resting in the back seat of the car and I could not move.

She quickly unhooked her seatbelt and rushed to my side. I still could not move. She took off my seatbelt but all I could do was just lay there with my head against the headrest and my hands on the steering wheel. Continuously she assured me that I was not alone, that I would be all right.

Seriously Injured

Soon, the ambulance arrived and after refusing any aid, Julie insisted that they treat me first. She watched in horror as they literally pulled me by the belt of my pants onto a back board and taped my head down. She was allowed to ride in the front of the ambulance only and all she could do was to watch from her vantage point as they poked my legs and feet with a sharp instrument and asked me if I could feel it. Unfortunately, the feeling had not returned to my body from the neck down.

After arriving at the hospital, I was whisked away behind a locked door to the treatment area. For nearly two hours they examined me and all the while Julie sat in the waiting area unable to see me or know anything that was going on in my treatment room.

Shortly, the Highway Patrol officer came through the door to take her report.

"What about the blue car?" he asked.

"Oh, you mean the one that was stopped?" she replied.

"Well, I guess that's all for now," he said closing his notebook.

You see, she had seen the car in front of us appear to be stopped and had also seen several people around the outside of the car. She assumed that they had a flat tire and were fixing it. Only later did she realize that no one would be fixing a flat in the middle of the fast traffic lane when there was a huge median area. The Officer had apparently thought that she was in shock because of her answer to his request for information regarding the blue car and abruptly ended his questioning after only two or three questions.

An eyewitness report to the Highway Patrol officers and later confirmed by a personal call to the party by us stated that the blue car, called a phantom car by the Highway Patrol, had preceeded us into the dirt median area and as soon as we came to a stop, it proceeded to dart out of the area, head down the highway and disappear from sight. Keep in mind that this is a long, straight stretch of road and the distance you could see up ahead was quite far.

The young man told us that he himself couldn't understand why that blue car had gone into the dirt area before us and had darted out as soon as we stopped. But we knew.

MIB Return

Once again, the "men in black" had tried to put us out of commission. And once again they had failed.

My wife was totally distraught be the time they finally let her in to see me. This was approximately five hours after our arrival at the hospital. All that time, she sat alone, in a strange hospital, behind a locked door, surrounded by strangers who knew nothing of either one of us. All she could think about was that her husband might be dying and noone was even back there in the treatment room praying for him.

"I'm sorry I wrecked the car," I said as she approached the bed where I lay awaiting my ride to the x-ray department.

"Who cares about the car?" she replied as she walked to my side and gently kissed my lips.

The Highway Patrol officer was still standing there and tried to caution her about touching me, but she would not be stopped. Tears filled her eyes as she saw me helpless, flat on my back. They allowed her to stay only a few moments before they took me upstairs for further tests. I kissed her again and back she went to the waiting area not knowing when she would see me again and what my condition would be.

As we approached the radiology department, I saw a familiar figure. After asking the technicians to leave the room in his inimitable fashion, Val approached the head of my bed and placed his hands on either side of my head.

"Frank, don't worry. Do not say anything. Everything will be all right," he said.

His words sounded like the song of angels and I closed my eyes while I heard him pray that God would perform another healing miracle for one of His children.

As quickly as he had appeared, he was gone. I felt a warm, tingly sensation throughout my entire body. The technicians returned and x-rayed me from head to toe. It would be several hours before I would return to the emergency treatment area. By that time the miracle had been fulfilled and I was allowed to get up and get dressed.

I could see the grave disappointment on the face of the attending physician. I had overheard him earlier discussing the financial aspects of my case. Suffice it to say that the dollar signs had left his eyes and he shook his head in utter dismay. A few minutes later, Julie would finally be allowed to see me again and together we walked out to the front desk to "check out".

Amazing Recovery

As we passed an open door, inside we could see the same ambulance drivers who brought us in. They had apparently brought in another person.

When they saw me upright, walking out, they both did a double take and one said, "You mean your neck's not broken?".

"You mean your hip's not broken?" said the other in amazement.

They could not believe their eyes seeing me walk out of that hospital so soon under my own steam, arm in arm with my wife. She had actually refused treatment to make sure that the paramedics and the doctors at the hospital attended me first. This would not be a decision she would ever make again because accepting treatment for herself would have at least gotten her in back of the locked door and in the same area where I was.

We smiled at the two who had been so kind to us and assured them that I was indeed all right now. They continued to shake their heads still not believing what they were seeing with their eyes.

We called a taxi to return us to our hotel. The car had not been drivable and had been towed to the car dealer for repair. That night I was able to go aboard Victor One for further treatments and a more complete explanation of what had taken place.

Please keep in mind that shortly before this incident took place, Julie and I had celebrated our marriage and we were in the area on our honeymoon. We had been there only two days when this incident took place. By the time the next morning came, she was in quite a bit of pain from her own injuries and still very shaken by the entire incident. It would be three days later, in the middle of the night, that I would awaken to hear her crying at the thought that someone actually wanted us permanently removed from this life. She had been hearing stories of the "men in black" for many years but this was the first time she had personal knowledge. Unfortunately, it would not be her last.

Special Protection

Because of the impact of this incident on our lives, I was informed by Commander Val that the time was now right for certain knowledge to be given to me to share with others.

This information is the RING OF FIRE prayer and ceremony which Val told me that he and his people perform before they ever set foot on this planet. I will inform you now of a segment of Divine Order that was established before the very foundation of this planet was laid.

The words which you are about to read are "absolute" in all respects. The mysterious "Ring of Fire" will become a vital part of your life. It is an essential part of one's walk on the path to true light and provides you with a cloak of protection never before made available. Almighty God has made provision to change our hearts and minds. It is up to each of us to adopt these changes in our lives.

Prince of the Air

Since the war in heaven, Lucifer and his band of angels (a full one third of the heavenly host) were cast down INTO the planet Earth. Holy writings, throughout the ages, have testified that this planet has been held captive by him and that he is in fact the prince of the powers of the air. It is under his influence that the atmosphere which you now breathe has become polluted with health-threatening particles. Every evil that is committed on Earth today can be traced to the influence of Lucifer and his crew. The level of crime, the disharmony, the disunity, man's inhumanity to man...all these under his evil influence.

Because of this, those from other planets are instructed to perform a ceremony called the "Ring of Fire". Although performed by a few in Bible days, the threats of the early Church kept this information hidden from the people until very few now know of its power.

Divine Protection

There is a formula by which all of you can benefit from the Divine Protection which results from this ceremony. Some of you may even take issue with the manner in which this power is invoked. But that is immaterial. The Name in which the invocation is pronounced may cause friction. But I will inform you of this great truth without reservation. The proof is in the pudding, so to speak. The "formula" has withstood the test of time. If our friends from space invoke this Divine Protection before ever setting foot on this planet, can we be so complacent as to not afford ourselves the same opportunity? Will you allow the evil forces to continue their deeds of destruction to every phase of life on Earth until there is nothing left? Or will you maintain an open mind and accept the freedom and protection that is offered to you here?

Fire has always been representative of Divine Protection, cleansing and purification. Far too many people are dying before their time while others are suffering unnecessary sickness and disease. UFO researchers are increasingly becoming targets of the ungodly forces which permeate our world. Even the Governments are deceiving the people into believing lies. In view of these facts, do you or do you not, need to be surrounded by the "Ring of Fire"?

A Ritual You Can Perform

Please follow these instructions carefully:
1. Place a lighted white candle before you on a table or other flat surface. Be careful to place a dish or other object under the candle to catch any drips.

2. Under no circumstances should you permit anyone or anything to interrupt you while you are performing this ceremony.
3. Recite The Lord's Prayer.
4. Pray the following prayer without doubt in your heart. Believe that the God of Creation is hearing you at the very moment that you are praying! Keep your eyes open as you pray, lifting your outstretched hands heavenward. Look into the flame and maintain your full senses. Know what you are doing at all times. Repeat aloud...

"Eternal Father, Creator of the Universe... Hear this day my petition. Surround me NOW...with your Divine Ring of Fire... The Fire of Your Protection...The Fire of Your Abundance...The Fire of Complete Healing...The Fire of Divine Abundance.

I now command the Hand of Almighty God on my behalf...Let it be so...this very moment...In the Blessed Name of the Lord Jesus Christ. Amen."

Now, as you look into the flame of the candle, place ALL your heartfelt desires as well as your problems, into the flame. Extinguish the candle and watch the smoke rising as to the nostrils of God as He receives your prayers. Do not remove yourself from the room for at least three full minutes. As you stand before the extinguished candle, keep your eyes open and feel the presence of the "Ring of Fire". You can perform this prayer/ceremony anywhere, anytime. Even while driving your car, you can pronounce the words and feel the protection of the "Ring of Fire". You will never be the same again.

Chapter Eight
Spacecraft Over Earth

(Special thanks to Mr. Robert Hover for his contribution to this chapter.)

Parked near the shore of the western-most reach of Lake Mead, east of Las Vegas, Nevada, is VICTOR ONE, a spacecraft from an extraterrestrial culture in which the name Commander Valiant Thor is prominent. This is the craft which he commands and uses as his "home" on Earth. VICTOR ONE is northwest of hoover Dam, southeast of Nellis Air Force Base, northeast of the town of Henderson, Nevada, and south of the Gypsum Plant. As of early December, 1988, it was just south of Las Vegas Wash about a mile northeast of the junction of Highways 147 and 166. It can move about. VICTOR ONE has been in this vicinity for eleven years. There are other Victor Class spacecraft which have been observing Earth for thousands of years. Several thousand people of Earth know of VICTOR ONE...approximately 2000 are U.S. Government officials currently in office. A limited number of people of Earth have visited VICTOR ONE, including several scientists. No government officials have ever visited VICTOR ONE.

The "Victor Class" Sector

A spacecraft of the Victor Class is a 300-foot diameter discus, twenty-two feet high at the rim, increasing to ninety-seven feet on the axis. The permanent crew is approximately 200. Its audio-visual-laser-type camera can select and pick up any person's actions and words as well as record them, all this up to a distance of 1200 miles from the spacecraft. There are presently about 450 persons under surveillance by VICTOR ONE. Only 20% are of a positive nature. The rest present some kind of threat to the planet.

Approximately 103 Victor Class spacecraft are on or near the surface of the Earth, active between some 287 locations. The first Victor Class ship visited Earth nearly 6,000 years ago. When Albert Einstein's four papers of technical development first appeared in 1905, the need for close scrutiny increased. Deployment reached the present level of 103 in 1981 during the peak threat of nuclear war.

All of the Victor Class ships were carefully constructed on board the Starship. There is a level compartment on the very bottom of the Starship where these ships are constructed and housed until they are dispatched. The crews are carefully chosen with the ranking officers being those who are considered seasoned to command such a craft. The design of the Victor Class ships is constant. There are no variations. There are other scout ships that are smaller (such as the one which Val used to go to Alexandria, Virginia and visit the Pentagon). These have a capacity of one, two, three, four, six, eight or ten persons. All of these are also constructed of the same basic material as the Victor Class ships. The shapes vary. As a matter of fact, they have been built in every shape known to man. A mini-class ship with an elongated configuration in the shape of a torpedo is used to transport supplies. These are those which have been seen coming out of the sides of mountains in California, Nevada and Arizona. Bases inside these mountain areas house these craft as well. You may have heard some of the stories the Indians tell of these bases.

All of the Victor Class ships have the capability of interplanetary travel if and when it's necessary. However, for the

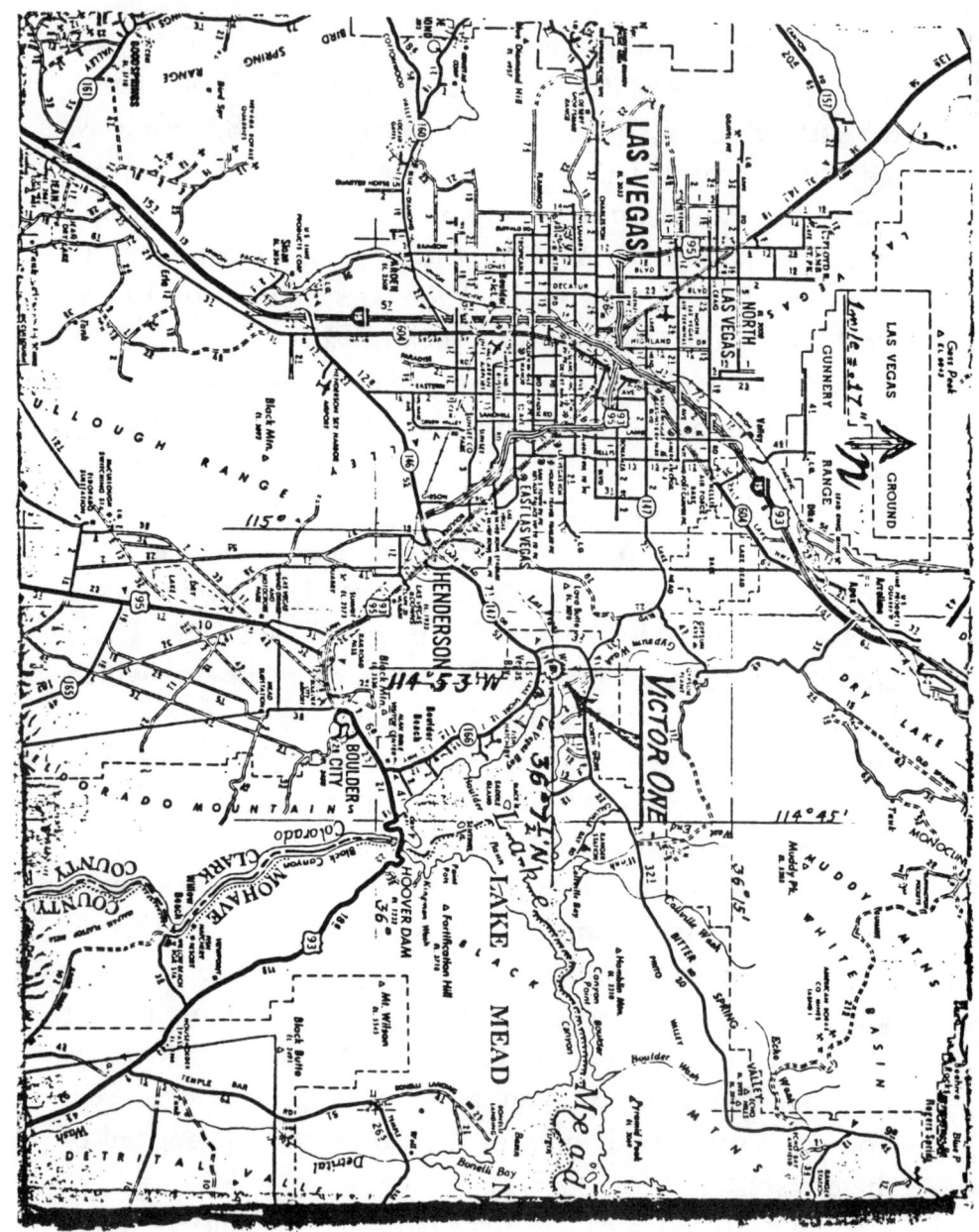

Location of "Victor One" in Las Vegas.

most part, they are used only on and around the Earth and Moon. The smaller ships are not designed for deep space travel. Commander Val was instrumental in the original design of the Victor ships.

Propulsion Secrets

The secret of propulsion in VICTOR ONE lies in the proper use of vibration. In every one of the Victor Series ships there is a "POWER ROD" that governs propulsion. Utilizing the power of electromagnetism, the ship is able to draw from this power which is then circulated through the navigational system without worrying about a breakdown in the system because it actually is capable of repairing itself. With the knowledge that all forces are vibratory (some high, some low), the high nullifies or repels the lower one against which it is opposed. In most cases, the higher is the dominating force. The length and rapidity of the waves are governed by the initial vibrations of the force. This force also forms an impenetrable shield around the ship which in turn repels anything that may be in its pathway. Thus if they should encounter any space junk or even a meteor bombardment while in flight, the "force field" will cause it to disintegrate and it will be reduced to a fine powder.

The entire "force field" is so simplistic that many of our top scientists and space engineers would stumble over its uncomplicated structure. A "force field" is created by a combination of magnetism and electricity which is diverted in order to exert power to resist magnetization or demagnetization. The on-board computer operates this power and by displacing the "forces" outside the ship, they are able to achieve the following results...invisibility and unhampered space flight.

Lines of Force

The universe is alive with interacting magnetic lines of force. The basic structure of the skin of the ship is very thin thus allowing the on-board mechanisms to operate without hindrance. It is made of a substance similar to a plastic-crystal matter. Some layers are positive-ionized, some are negative. These are insulated from each other with neutral layers between them. Due to the fact that cosmic rays in space are unstable, the ship's operation through space in not affected. In reality, what we are witnessing is a marvelous harmony and cooperation with natural forces. There are endless variations of magnetic fields or fluxes in the universe. Cosmic rays produce their own magnetic wakes in their paths. Thus the "ether" is in constant motion at all times in all places. The crystal property of the Victor series refines all the electro-magnetic and corpuscular energies into varying frequencies and wave lengths.

Cosmic rays actually represent various forms of radiation of intense penetrating power and high frequency, impinging upon the planet Earth from outer space and subdivided into high energy "primary rays" consisting almost entirely of positively-charged particles. Also, secondary rays formed from many types of atomic particles, positive and negative in charge. These charges, because of their nature, are not constant and are very unstable. This condition exists not only around the Earth but also in all of the material universe.

As the crystal property is stepped up by the electro-magnetic energy, its lattice structure undergoes certain changes which cause the ship to emit light of various colors. When such a force is discharged under normal conditions, a flame or darting lightning is visible all around the ship. Thus we see streaks of fire. In some cases, even a vapor trail emitting from the direction from which the ship has come. By directing a sudden impulse of energy and resistance to the energy simultaneously into the ship, it can be made to explode into a shower of spark fragments... This is only done under controlled conditions.

Master Beam

The Victor Series ships are not just guided but completely controlled at all times. The master beam from the Starship holds each of these ships locked in like a vise. Every molecule and every atom is vectored in the same direction at the same time. Any gravitational effects from inertia are thereby neutralized or non-existent. The air forces of the world governments as well as their scientists are in a quandary as they try to explain how these ships operate, violating every known law of aerodynamics. Because of the magnetic lines of force in space which frequently cross each other, the ship easily rides these lines thus executing impossible right angle turns WITHOUT SLOWING DOWN.

There are times when the wings of our own dulled imaginations fail to grasp the reality that we are dealing with HIGHLY ADVANCED beings with ADVANCED knowledge and instrumentation that WE ourselves would command if only certain individuals from the beginning of recorded history had not dropped the ball.

Locations of the Ships

The 287 locations of the Victor Series ships by land masses, oceans or countries are as follows:

North & South Pacific Ocean 38
Japan 29
USA (48 States)..21
North & South Atlantic Ocean.............................18
USSR..17
China & Mongolia 17
India, Afghanistan through Viet Nam 17
Middle East 17
Africa & Madagascar 17
Europe..15
Indian Ocean...13
Philippines & Indonesian Islands 11
Australia & New Zealand....................................9
South America...8
Scandanavia 7
Canada 6
Korea..5
Arctic Ocean 4
Greenland & Iceland 3
Central America 2
Antarctica 2
Alaska 1
Others (due to vagueness of boundaries 10

The total number of crew on VICTOR ONE, as previously mentioned, is 200. With Valiant Thor as Commander, there are four crew members who serve in the capacity of

Vice Commander. These include Donn, Thonn, Teel and the Medical Officer who is known as "Doc". These commanders have been chosen to serve until further advised. The rest of the compliment are those from the home planet Venus who have elected to serve under the direct command of Commander Val Thor. From time to time, however, there are those from other systems who volunteer to serve on VICTOR ONE for short periods of time...about three Earth months. This is done so that those of the crew members who wish to return home for a time may do so without disrupting the vital functions of the ship. Remember, life is not the same on other planets as it is here on Earth. No person or job is looked upon as any more or less important than any other person or job. All are happy to be in the service of The Creator and perform any function which HE may choose for them. Of course, everyone looks with eyes of great respect and admiration upon Val Thor and other commanders because of their knowledge that Val and his Vice Commanders have been DIRECTLY APPOINTED BY THE MASTER TO THEIR POSITIONS.

Cosmic Teachings

Three to five crew members directly assist V.C. Teel in the preparation and teaching of the various classes conducted aboard VICTOR ONE. Most of these classes are conducted by her and pertain directly to the following subjects:

A. Earth Sciences
B. Earth people and their habits
C. The fall of mankind and the Salvation of Jesus Christ
D. The psychology of the human being

E. The reason for the human being

F. The history of mankind

G. The ultimate position of mankind in the universe.

Teel often uses as examples a few Earth people. For example, my wife Julie is a popular subject in her classes. These classes are conducted for both outer space and Earth visitors to VICTOR ONE and are conducted five days per week.

It may interest you to know that every morning a meeting is conducted to give worship to The Master Creator. Commander Val, when he is present, speaks briefly to everyone...usually complimenting visitors and welcoming newcomers, many of whom have assisted crew members in the performance of their duties. Usually visitors lend a helping hand and thereby learn what tasks must be performed on VICTOR ONE on a daily basis. Whenever Val or one of his crew leave VICTOR ONE for any reason, they are in constant communication with the ship and can be called to return in the event of an emergency. Depending on the scope of the emergency, they will either return with their vehicle or will be beamed aboard.

The "POWER ROD" which runs from the top to the bottom of the ship is located directly in the center of VICTOR ONE. This rod also powers the defense mechanism in the form of advanced laser-type equipment. It is from this rod that the laboratory and the medical treatment rooms are powered.

Communications Systems

There are three main communications systems aboard all

Victor Ships. They are:

1. TELEPATHIC: The individual communication officer has achieved an advanced level of development of telepathic ability. His power is virtually limitless in this area. Most communication between ships and/or ground personnel is sent and received in this manner.

There are special devices on board called TAXTO which controls the "beam lock" that allows the ship to remain on a true course at all times. The telepathic ability of the operator (pilot) with which he also controls the TAXTO device is a vital part of every extraterrestrial. This type of communication is sometimes utilized when communicating with those of planet Earth as well as crew members who are outside the Victor Ship.

Not all communication between space people and those of Earth is done by man-made transmitters and receivers involving complicated electronic circuits and bulky equipment. When communication of this nature is accomplished without the aid of a single electronic component, this phenomena is commonly referred to as "mental telepathy". One form radiates brain waves as far as they are sent without concern for negative obstruction. Vibrations such as this travel completely around the planet, as fast as the speed of thought. When this thought wave pattern strikes another brain which is keyed to the same vibratory rate, the receiver brain understands perfectly the thought waves from the person sending the message. This includes the person operating a spacecraft. Therefore, with TWO points "keyed" to the same vibration, it is perfectly easy to execute thought waves to a person or thought waves to an instrument or mechanism.

2. HOLOGRAPHIC: When it become necessary for a "visual" contact, the hologram has proven to be the most effective. In this manner, the person can actually "see" the one who is transmitting the message. This is the same system which is located in the "personal residence bases" which I described to you in an earlier chapter.

The hologram is actually a photographic process utilizing a split-beam of laser light in order to produce on a photographic plate, minus the necessity of using a lens. In other words, the interference pattern of light waves. This results in a three-dimensional image that can be captured by a receiving device and then reconstructed and viewed. The most advanced type of holographic equipment is a system whereby both sender and receiver can carry on a two-way conversation, as is the case with the certain locations on our planet. Keep in mind that these communications are like ACTUALLY being there and are in full color.

3. DIRECT COMMUNICATION: This represents simply the ability of extraterrestrials to reroute their audio/visual ability to communicate with those of Earth through a radio, television set and telephone. This is the method utilized by Commander Val and others from time to time in their communications with me.

When certain people are in constant communication with space beings, there is often no need for special equipment in order to maintain a steady link-up. They are able to utilize whatever we have in our homes, offices, cars, etc. I have personally walked by a telephone booth somewhere, the telephone rings and it is Val on the other end of the line wishing to converse with me. I have also witnessed his communicating with me through my car radio even when it was not on. Communication is easily accomplished by those who are called Angels of God.

It is Donn who most frequently visits the Los Angeles area traveling to the residence of his long-time friend, Dr. Lee, to discuss world conditions, relate news of some of Dr. Lee's friends in Japan and Hong Kong, meet other visitors, as well as enjoy their company. This also gives me the opportunity to meet with him personally and receive his counsel in matters pertaining to my life and my work.

Donn generally accompanies me on my travels within the United States as well as around the world. This too gives us the opportunity to converse at length. The confines of a jet flying at 35,000 feet provides each of us with a captive audience as well as a relaxing, uninterrupted atmosphere.

Truly a great work is being performed before us if only we have the eyes to see, the ears to hear and the faith to believe.

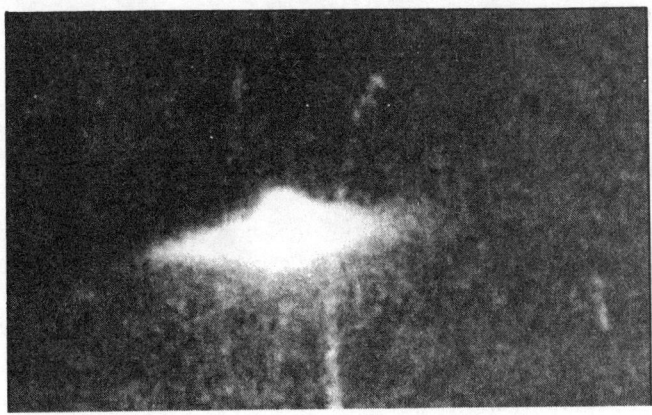

Space craft over Andes

"Bell-shaped" UFO taken in 1972, over Grants Pass, Oregon, by Tahahlita.

Epilogue

Any student of holy writings must readily admit that man condemns himself by ignoring the truths which have been set out in the Word of God. Ample provision has been made for the benefit of mankind on this planet. Healing and a deeper Spiritual experience are readily available for man to enjoy. For those who have chosen to believe by faith, signs and wonders will follow them. God still maintains "His" order despite man's plans and predictions. This holds true today as it has for all time.

Those who have constantly refused to walk in the light, having a knowledge of that light, yet persisting in evil thoughts and deeds, shall never see the glory of paradise. The world is already witnessing the powerful Hand of God in action. The doubters and mockers would have you deny these mighty works. But in days to come, the meek, the humble, the honest truth-seekers will find that a closer walk with God will indeed produce great and far reaching dividends.

There are horizons the height and depth of which have thus far been unexplored. The Hand of God has extended far beyond that which our feeble minds can comprehend. There are scopes of Spiritual science and research that have not been explored because of fear and superstition.

Nevertheless, the Lord has promised to lead and guide us into ALL TRUTH by His Spirit. We are privileged to live in the time of awareness of angelic visitors. This is His sign of His Love for us. Let Him who is the Author of Peace strike that harmonious chord that will quell the trembling of your hearts. Do not be troubled concerning wars, bombs, missiles, international or national difficulties. Think pure thoughts and walk with Him. The provision He has made for each and every one of us is available not only through His ever-present Spirit, but also through His Word and the writings of those who have learned the truth and whose hearts beat to the same universal rhythm.

Many years ago, during several of Val's visits with the people of Earth, certain information was given which has benefited all who have read it with an open mind and heart and applied its truth to their own lives. These lessons are contained in the book OUTWITTING TOMORROW which I urge to you read. This gift remains timely to this day and will endure until the Earth is changed and new. My earnest prayer is that you may receive that which God has for you in these days. May God bless you, dear reader, always.

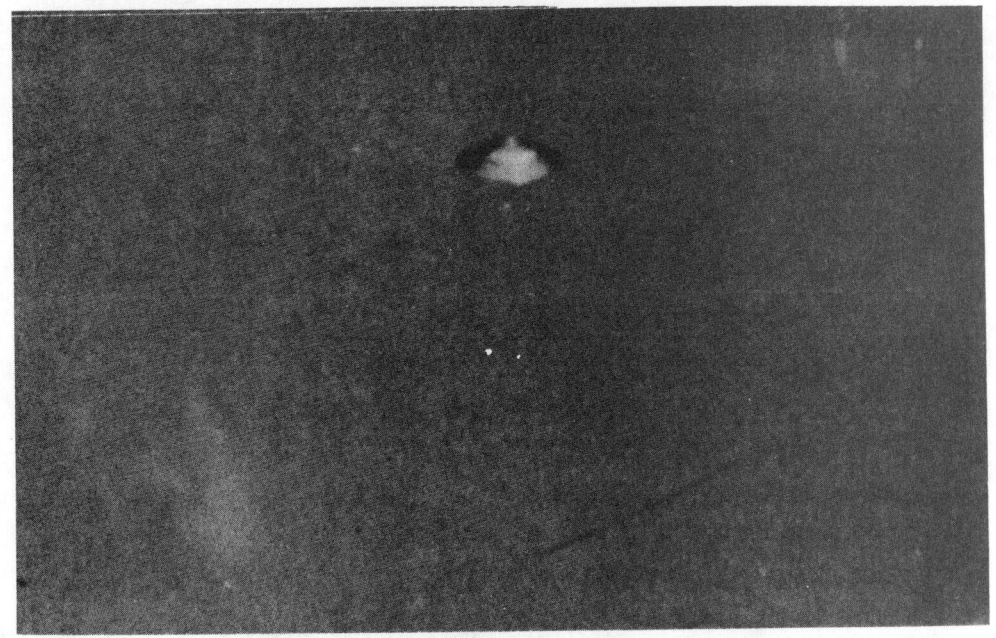

South of France.

A Final Word from Valiant Thor

Those of you who are reading this book will know the truth. The very fact that you are open to truth is amply reflected in your interest in this book. It is no accident that you have come in contact with Dr. Frank Stranges. If you, as a student, are ready for the whole truth, he will teach you.

Be prepared to launch out into areas of research and investigation that will excite your high consciousness such as never before. Reevaluate your personal goals and seek to change them for the better, accordingly. Remember, YOU must be the one to change.

You have been reminded that success and prosperity must be experienced FIRST in the mind, then it will become a REALITY. Let me also state the importance of your overall contribution of love, time and devotion to service. Loyalty to your Overseer who is Christ along with the unselfish gift of your substance can only result in heavenly treasure.

Once you have made your commitment to the Master, keep that commitment. To forfeit it is to break your word. It is called your love tithe to God. Do not be surprised that I mention this.

In fulfilling this commitment you will be counted as worthy in God's eyes to be one CHOSEN for a specific task. To deny yourself this will also hamper your Spiritual growth. Begin to place yourself in the position of a LEADER instead of a follower. The decision is clearly up to you.

Many wonder why God is using you, mankind, to perpetuate His will. This thought was established from the beginning. You are a part of that plan—if you so choose. Let your mind be permeated by the Divine Mind and you will work exploits in His Name.

Frank E. Stranges, Ph.D.

Many have requested that I come and lecture, conduct classes, teach you what I know. This is quite impossible. However, through Dr. Stranges, a vehicle has been designed to fulfill that request.

It would not be practical for you to expect me to come to teach you individually or collectively at this time as I must perform the following tasks in my position:

1. Command the Starship as well as VICTOR ONE
2. Head the Venusian Council of Twelve
3. Control certain outposts around this planet
4. Oversee the task forces used to contain radiation around your cities
5. Make regular journeys to and from the planets
6. Conduct seminars on the Starship for the indoctrination of those visiting from other star systems
7. Monitor discussion and plans by world leaders
8. Prevent atomic holocaust by exercising certain limits on certain human agencies
9. Work in full harmony with our Heavenly Creator

Please do remember that there are at this time seven persons, of various backgrounds and experience on this Earth who have been gifted with a keen insight regarding matters pertaining to the future of this planet. It would do you good to listen to these four men and three women, one of whom is Dr. Frank Stranges. The others will make themselves known to their groups in their respective parts of the globe.

In conclusion, please remember to keep God's Word. Seek to do good. Think thoughts of purity and godliness. You can change yourself for good and thereby the world will change. Do not be guilty of ignorance or avoidance of the Perfect Will of God.

I leave you with my love. God bless you and God keep you, always perfect in His Ways.

Frank E. Stranges, Ph.D.

Postscript: Signs and Wonders

Many letters have been received at my headquarters in Van Nuys, California, wanting me to make predictions based upon my conversations with Commander Valiant Thor. And while Valiant does not claim to be a seer, in keeping with his "projections" of current trends and based upon my own interpretations of scripture, it is possible to tell certain things about events that we are likely to see happen in the not-too-distant future.

The next global conflict I believe will develop in the Middle East, where we have already seen much conflict, death and disaster. This future conflict will likely involve Israel, the Arab states, the countries of Western Europe, the USSR and the United States. Here is the order of events as they will transpire in the Last Days!

1. MILLIONS WILL VANISH FROM THE FACE OF THE EARTH.
2. CHILDREN WILL BE REPORTED MISSING (remember the prediction that the Space Brothers will take our youngsters first), LOVED ONES GONE, GRAVES OPENED.
3. DISTRESS OF NATIONS, SUCH AS NEVER BEFORE TRANSPIRED ON THIS PLANET.
4. TRANSPORTATION WILL BE A MAJOR

PROBLEM.
5. FROM THIS POINT ON, A SERIES OF PRESIDENTIAL ORDERS WILL BE ISSUED TO THE AUTHORITIES ON THIS PLANET, PLACING EVERY LIVING PERSON IN THE U.S. UNDER COMPLETE DICTATORSHIP!
6. ONCE THE "CHOSEN" HAVE BEEN REMOVED, THE PRESIDENT WILL:
   A. Take over all communications media.
   B. Take over all petroleum, gas, fuel, electric power, etc.
   C. Take over all food resources, farms, etc.
   D. Take over all modes of transportation, highways, airports.
   E. Mobilize all civilians into work forces under government supervision.
   F. Take over all health, welfare and education.
   G. Postmaster authorized to conduct nationwide registration of ALL persons.
   H. Take over all airplanes, aircraft, including private planes.
   I. Take over all housing, financing—to relocate people, build with public funds in certain designated areas.

Furthermore, scientists agree that there will be drastic weather changes; fierce changing winds: rapidly accelerating solar activity connected with an outward gravitational pull that may cause the earth to become exceedingly hot for several days; the ice caps may melt and earthquakes occur all over the earth. If the predictions of the scientists measure up to even 26 percent of expectations, then soon there may be a time of desolation and tribulation. Jesus said of His coming again, as recorded in Luke 21:25–28, that there would be *fearsome signs in the heavens and upon the earth, distress of nations.*

Since 1945, the world has witnessed on several occasions the rising of pillars of smoke and fire into the atmosphere from the explosion of nuclear devices. Joel said this would be one of the signs of the last days.

As we have already brought out, earthquakes will be only a part of the drastic environmental changes on earth that scientists believe will take place. However, earthquakes are perhaps the most important from a Biblical standpoint, because earthquakes have always signified dispensation changes in God's dealings with mankind. There must have been great earthquakes at the flood, because we read in Genesis 7:11...*that the fountains of the great deep were broken up.* There must have been another great earthquake at the time that God divided the nations at the time of the Tower of Babel. God divided the nations by race, languages, and cultures; and He divided them by mountains, rivers, seas, deserts and oceans. Science has now verified that the continents were all one huge land mass, but something happened and they broke up and floated apart. For example, the east coast of South America fits like a puzzle piece against the west coast of Africa. And if you will consult an earthquake map of the fault lines around the world, they generally follow the coasts of the continents, indicating that a great earthquake most likely caused the continents and islands to separate.

Other Books by Dr. Frank E. Stranges

UFO CONSPIRACY
NAZI UFO SECRETS AND BASES EXPOSED
THE WHITE PLANET
MYSTERY MAN OF DARKNESS #666
THE STAR OF BETHLEHEM
OUTWITTING TOMORROW (by Valiant Thor)
For a full catalog of books and audio/video tapes, write to:
I.E.C.—BOOK/TAPE DEPT.
P.O. Box 73
VAN NUYS, CA 91408-0073
(818) 989-5942